THE

MILLENNIAL

MERGER

How to Sell, Manage, Empathize, and Communicate
in a Multi-Generational Workforce

JESSE HENRY

The Millennial Merger

How to Sell, Manage, Empathize, and Communicate in a Multi-Generational Workforce

Published By: The Theory of Success, LLC

For more information, please go to www.JesseHenry.co.

For Inquiries, email JesseHenry4@gmail.com

Manufactured in the United States of America.

ISBN: 978-1-7324137-2-6 paperback

ISBN: 978-1-7324137-1-9 eBook

To Mom and Dad,

for creating an extroverted introvert.

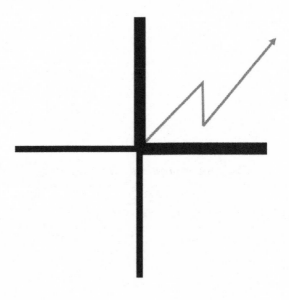

Table Of Contents

◼ Acknowledgements

Before this book begins, I'd like to acknowledge the 17 people who were murdered at the Marjory Stoneman Douglas High School shooting on February 14, 2018.

Coach Aaron Feis, Jamie Guttenberg, Chris Hixon, Alyssa Alhadeff, Scott Beigel, Martin Anguiano, Nicholas Dworet, Luke Hoyer, Cara Loughran, Gina Montalto, Joaquin Oliver, Alaina Petty, Helena Ramsay, Alex Schachter, Carmen Schentrup, Meadow Pollack, and Peter Wang.

Stoneman Douglas High School, Westglades Middle School, and the cities of Parkland and Coral Springs Florida provided a picture-perfect place for me to grow up. My formative years were full of opportunity, support, and most importantly, safety. Ironically, Parkland was named the safest town in Florida. But, somehow, Douglas became the site of the deadliest high school shooting in American history. What were the chances?

That school is part of my identity – it's part of my soul. Those teachers and coaches relentlessly pushed me to better myself. That community supported me when the going got tough. Those classrooms helped build me into the man I am today.

Unfortunately, the town where I grew up became a national icon for all the wrong reasons.

People like Aaron Feis, the football coach who put himself between bullets and students, represents the greatest virtues a human can possess: courage, integrity, and honor. The man died exactly as he lived. The same could be said for many, if not all, of the victims at Douglas High School.

When we look at a situation like this, we must ACKNOWLEDGE that holistic problems cannot be solved using reductionistic methodologies.

"This is bigger than a mental illness issue. This is bigger than a semi-automatic weapons issue. This is bigger than a background check issue. This is bigger than a school safety issue. This is bigger than a bullying issue. This is bigger than a parenting issue."

This is an American issue. No other country on the planet faces mass murders at the rate we do.

That is something we must all ACKNOWLEDGE.

When we face trying times, we look to politicians to create policy and legislation that removes the friction from our lives. If politicians continue to represent the lobbyists and corporate interests of their puppeteers, they will NOT be reelected. If they are, then I fear our democracy might truly be broken. Millennials don't care about partisanship – they care about change.

It's become increasingly apparent that the partisan structure of our government and public sector will be challenged as the new generations exceed the 35-year-old threshold. If there's one thing you can count on, it's that many of the policies implemented by our elders will be amended to fit within the social structure of the 21st century.

Thoughts and prayers are not enough, and, a cliché resolution at best.

Something within me tells me that Parkland Florida will be the epicenter of a movement. I've seen what this tragedy has done to the place I called home for so long. The people of Parkland have a fire in their eyes. These kids are eloquent, logical, and most importantly, willing to go to the ends of the earth to attain the change they seek. Just watch the recordings online.

These kids are just old enough to recognize the negligence of our politicians, and just young enough to tirelessly commit to change.

We must ACKNOWLEDGE that America's #1 priority needs to be the protection and prosperity of its citizens.

We must ACKNOWLEDGE that changing times call for changing measures.

And, we must ACKNOWLEDGE that the path we're currently on is unsustainable.

Mark my words – Stoneman Douglas students, alumni, and the City of Parkland Florida, will be the change we wish to see in the world. You can count on it.

#EaglePride

■ Foreword

By: Brad Szollose

I was startled a bit as gunshots rang out across the open loft space of our offices at 55 Broad Street in New York City. Having learned to fire a rifle in the Boy Scouts by the time I was 12, I was familiar with *real* gunfire. This was something else.

As I rounded the corner into our conference room, there at the end of an 18-foot long conference room table was John Balestrieri playing a vigorous round of Doom (an online first-person shooter game). At the time, *Doom* was a huge leap forward in online gaming due to texture mapping and a true 3D world. The 36" monitor and Infinity speakers brought the graphics and sound effects to life.

Immediately, my baby boomer brain went to *"why is he playing a video game? Aren't video games for kids?"*

Startled by my entrance, John didn't miss a beat as he yelled,

"Sorry. I thought I was the only one here."

John didn't just work for me, I considered him a friend and a technology wiz. Give him 6 months and he could learn any and every programming language inside and out. Since John went way beyond the call of duty for our clients, if he wanted to play an online video game late at night to relax, I was fine with it.

Stealthily moving from one room to the next. Reloading. Firing. Boom. More gunfire. John continued yelling, explaining to me how he was beating the pants off a group of players in France.

I yelled back... "Well of course you're beating them..." I chuckled, "...you're on a T1 line."

John burst out laughing as he glanced in my direction and leveled-up "yea...I feel sad for them." Most households in America had just started using 56K modems and here was John playing across the World Wide Web.

As I said my goodbyes and headed out the door, I started to realize the next generation had a completely different sense of work and play.

It was 1996 and this was my first descent into the world of generational issues.

I was the cofounder of one of the first Dot Com Agencies in the world. In 1995 my company, K2 Design, was listed by Advertising Age as one of 10 companies that could build websites for the big corporations. We built the IBM Deep Blue versus Garry Kasparov Chess Challenge for Ogilvy for 2 years in a row, along with building sites for MCI, Audi, American Express, Bell Atlantic, and many others.

Within 18 months of the Advertising Age article, we went from 2 business partners in a tiny set of offices, to 60 employees, offices worldwide, and an initial public offering (IPO) on NASDAQ. Our valuation was listed in the Wall Street Journal at $26 million.

That alone is a great story. But the real story is, I almost missed the Dot Com Boom! At first the Internet seemed to be a fad. A passing piece of tech that wasn't very robust. At first it seemed like nothing more than a glorified library. It was a slow burn, then suddenly the Internet became the greatest single thing since the printing press, landing on the moon, and the Great Pyramids of Giza.

But something else began to puzzle me at that time. As I mentioned before, I am a Baby Boomer. A Cusp Boomer to be exact raised on the ABC *Afterschool Special*, Disco Dancing and eventually 'new wave' bands like The Police.

A decade later, here I was working on the Internet and I started to notice something strange; my workforce, many of whom were only 3 to 10 years younger than me, were acting so differently from my generation, that I was forced to pay attention.

The warning signs were right in front of me. A new generation was pushing against everything I had been taught about people management. They told me off, wanted to work when they felt like it, showed up at 10:00 AM and demanded to work from home. And, they appeared to be hooked on technology.

Remote work and flex time are common methodologies today, but in 1996, they were highly disruptive.

To get this new digitally savvy workforce motivated required a complete shift in the way I managed people. I was forced to create a brand-new management model that satisfied all generations. Being a creative director, that was the easy part. In the design and advertising fields we manage people differently than an accounting firm. We expect people to make their deadlines on their own... like an adult.

Simply by treating people differently, and managing them as little as possible, we experienced 425% hypergrowth for 5 straight years with only 6% attrition! Of course, we trained people in the K2 way of working, but we did it all with no start-up capital. Our accounting firm interviewed everyone at K2, and was so astounded by the answers that they awarded us The Arthur Andersen Enterprise Award for fostering innovation amongst our employees.

As Buckminster Fuller stated "You never change the existing reality by fighting it. Instead, create a new model that makes the old one obsolete."

I became obsessed with figuring this generational paradox. Was it technology or parenting or something in the water? I exposed the top three influencers that changed the behavior of the next generations in my award-winning book, *Liquid Leadership.* But the key to understanding what is really going on is to realize that all generations to come will never be the same.

So why is *this* generational divide different than the hundreds of thousands that have happened before? Well, we've always had multiple generations in the workforce. When I was 16 in my first job, my grandfather was selling real estate. What makes today different is that all generations in the workforce have very different ideologies of how the world works best. The new generation also has a slew of different needs, wants, expectations, and behaviors than the generations that preceded them.

This generational divide is different because in the past, we all eventually assimilated into the previous generations way of thinking. Buying a house or having kids did that. But today we have a generation that was raised differently. Their thinking is different, and the tools they were raised with are different as well. This generational divide is permanent. No one is going back to that old way of thinking.

Just look at how much business training young people have had by playing video games (yes, you read that correctly). Learning to work with teams, mission-driven tasks, and realizing leadership is rotational and your team is comprised of those with the right skill sets. If you do not get up to speed fast enough, you are off the team. Leverage the technology and skills of your team members and win at any cost. Oh, and have fun while you invade the castle.

Sounds like business training to me.

Add to that, 2 generations that want a work/life balance. If you are a true leader of people in your organization, you know a train wreck is coming. As Boomers are forced into retirement, who will take over?

In the middle of this discord, a ray of sunshine has emerged. Jesse Henry has written an extraordinary book on how this cross-generational management model should work. *The Millennial Merger* is a powerful book that is needed right here, right now. It delves deeply into what makes each generation tick. Understanding "why" people act the way they do is just the beginning.

The command and control leadership model is over due to a simple fact; it requires employees to be malleable and obedient. Since anyone born after 1984 was not raised that way, the corporation must change to accommodate this. If they choose not to, then corporations around the world will have empty offices and transient workers.

Today, the art of persuasion is what works best.

For the majority of the Industrial Revolution, people were expected to be obedient workers. One of the very first management consultants, Frederick Winslow Taylor stated as much; "Workers have 2 inbuilt flaws: they are stupid like an ox, and they are lazy."

Some of that thinking can still be found in many a board room and executive suites today. It is toxic, and it is so out-of-date that these people should be on display in a museum.

Your average workforce has been taking apart and working with computers since childhood. They knew what a megabyte was at 4, and put together a LAN in their house while Dad was trying to program the VCR.

The new generations are highly educated, and diverse (both in race and gender). All of a sudden, it's becoming crystal clear that we're entering a world that older generations could have never imagined. A world where the smartest person in the organization may not be in the C-Suite, but may be the middle manager who can motivate 100 people with one sentence.

By the way, that Doom playing friend of mine, John, has moved on to become a partner in a gaming company and has developed a proprietary next generation gaming engine. He did that after becoming an executive at Sony and eventually starting his own airline.

I mention this because you have in front of you, a generation that has talent and potential that may not be seen with the naked eye at first. Especially if we continue to observe them through a Baby Boomer lens of expectations.

Many of my former employees went on to lead some of the most iconic organizations in the world, or became successful entrepreneurs launching their own software and cyber security firms.

I want you to get a highlighter and a pen. When you ask Jesse to sign your copy of *The Millennial Merger*, I expect the pages to be dog-eared, highlighted, underlined and the cover to be worn out.

THIS IS THE GUIDEBOOK we've been waiting for and didn't know it.

I am honored to be a part of Jesse's launch, and I hope this book sheds some much needed light on understanding each generation.

The best to you,

Brad Szollose

Global Business Advisor on Next Generation Leadership Development

Award-winning author of Liquid Leadership: From Woodstock to Wikipedia

TEDx Alum and Keynote Speaker *www.LiquidLeadership.com*

Why We Matter

◼ Introduction

Millennials: love 'em, hate 'em, idolize or demonize them it doesn't matter; you simply can't ignore them.

We've already transformed life as we know it and will continue to do so for the foreseeable future. There's some who cringe at the very thought, but this book is about embracing and leveraging that transformation.

The millennial generation (commonly referred to as Generation Y) is the group of individuals born between (approximately) 1980-2000 who ushered in the age of technology. They're sandwiched between Generation X, and Generation Z, who have their own unique perspectives about the world around them. Some researchers are even stating that there's a "micro-generation" called Xennial's who are born between 1977 and 1983. But, instead of focusing on specific birth dates, we're going to focus on psychological frameworks that are used by the different generations.

For better or for worse, millennials were the first to have computers as a cornerstone of their primary and secondary education. Generations not even born yet will read this book and look at millennials as the generation that buffered society from "the good ol' days" to "the new age. "With this new age of technology, a new way of thinking has evolved. This book is meant to outline the millennial ideology, which isn't necessarily confined to birthdates as much as it's tied to a way of thinking. The millennial philosophy affects politics, religion, business and communication as we know it. The following chapters will give insight to these shifts that have already changed the world.

We live in a society that's obsessed with transformation. Companies that have been in business throughout multiple generations are no better or worse off than a startup today. Changing times call for changing measures 21st century business is drastically different than the 'best practices' promoted in the 1900's. The playing field is as level as it's ever been, and it's all because of the rise of technology and the generation that's lived through it. Many big businesses think, *it's absurd to think that a generation will control how we do business.* Those companies are sadly mistaken.

If companies do not change and adapt to many of the new generations ideologies, failure will be a safe bet.

Some companies will adapt and thrive, and I hope that these insights help propel those organizations to new heights.

What *was*, what *is* and what *will be* are three different stories. Ever heard of the saying, "If you always do what you've always done, you'll always get what you've always gotten?" That statement doesn't necessarily hold true in this ever-changing economy.

Millennials don't adhere well to traditions. Just because it's always been done one way, doesn't mean it should still be done that way. Traditions are rules written by the ones before us. Although some traditions prove to be enlightening, there are those that only hold us back.

The path to success is based around our belief systems. And traditions within cultures create social constructs about what life should be – based on what was. What has proven to be successful in this modern era is the ability to change the beliefs that no longer serve us – to completely unleash from all social constructs and limitations in our lives. What we were told to believe, and what we need to believe to become successful may be two different stories. Most of our beliefs were installed into our brains when we were too young to make the choice for ourselves. We aren't born with political, religious, or corporate interests. Those beliefs were bestowed upon us by those who felt they were properly equipping us for the future. But, as we move forward, it's important we take a hard look at our beliefs to determine which ones drive us forward, which ones hold us back, and which ones fit into this modern world. We often forget that our perception shapes our reality. In this ever-changing world, it's important we adopt an open perspective to truly understand and appreciate the ideologies of others. We can only challenge our perspective of society by seeking to understand how others view the world. It's only then that we can determine whether their ideology is a perspective worth adopting.

This book was written to help *anyone* adopt the millennial mindset. As previously mentioned, this is an ideology; a new way of thinking. If you're looking to sell to, market to, manage, empower, communicate or befriend a millennial, it's important that you empathize with who we are and what we stand for.

Just like generations before us, millennials think and act based upon biological nature, and how they've been nurtured throughout life. There have been significant events and advances within society that have shaped this ideology and how we interact with others. This book contains the foresight necessary to not just survive, but to thrive in a society that's always looking for "the next big thing."

At the core of the millennial ideology is the concept of individualism. All humans have the need to feel special. Millennials are looking to change the world for the better, and they don't like to be herded into generalizations that demean them. Judge a millennial for who they are as an individual, not what you may think of them as a group. You'll realize that behind every millennial is a unique story that makes us different. Understand those disparities and you're on the road to success.

The purpose of this book is to provide some insight as to how companies (and individuals) can plan and adapt for the changes millennials will cause. I can promise you now that you may not agree with all the statements in this book, and that's okay. I'm not here to impose my beliefs on you, but to shed some light on conversations that look different today than they did yesterday. As you read *The Millennial Merger,* think about how you will adjust your personal philosophy and embrace change. No ideology is perfect and there's always room for improvement. Your perspective can help develop this way of thinking as it grows for years to come.

Generations (both present and future) all go through a "meeting of the minds" phase where collaboration feels unnatural. To improve your organization, *it's important to be able to understand this new age ideology, and empathize with the generation that helped segue society into the age of technological abundance.*

◼ Change

I n today's world, the only thing constant is change itself. Change is one of the most important parts of modern society it keeps the world on its toes. The millennial generation has welcomed change as part of societal growth and improvement. To fully embrace change, we must get comfortable with being uncomfortable. If we want to experience growth, we must become completely normalized with going outside of our comfort zone. How else can we expect to do more, be more, have more and achieve more? It all starts with that secret sauce called change!

Humans will always be fighting the double-edged sword between keeping consistent patterns and innovating new ones. Look, systems are great. They make us efficient, process-oriented and they create operational efficiencies (both personally and professionally). Implementing habits is how we attract success, but knowing when to change them is how we avoid failure. Challenging social norms from our past is what allows our society to thrive during times of change. Management techniques and company culture, as well as organized religion and politics have seen their traditions challenged to transform in the 21st century. What worked yesterday, what works today and what will work tomorrow are three things to be self-aware of at all times. Making the necessary changes in life is always a choice.

Every day we wake up, we make a choice a choice to live exactly as we did yesterday, or a choice to change and take a new action; a choice to let the external world dictate our internal world, or a choice to change and accept what we cannot control. The choices we make are based on the experiences we desire today, as well as our vision for brighter opportunities tomorrow.

Great executives don't just recognize opportunities, they create them. It's one of the most important characteristics of any successful company. To create opportunities in the 21st century, we must be willing to change. We can make a choice from the hand we've been dealt or we can develop a new opportunity to create a better hand. Millennials are always looking for ways to modernize the workplace, so organizations must make sure they're keeping up with the changing times.

Before we can implement change, we must become conscious of what needs changing. One of the most important steps we take in our lives is going from "not knowing what we don't know" to "knowing what we don't know." Some people face this step once a year, some once a week, some once a day and some once an hour. That curiosity to discover what we don't know will open the flood gates to change. But, the first step to change is discovering what we don't know.

Change can happen in an instant. Life is about constantly working to become the best version of ourselves at a specific moment. Martin Luther King, Nelson Mandela, Abraham Lincoln these people stepped into the moment, and took *that* specific step forward. It wasn't the step they should have taken the day before, or the step they needed to take the day after. They made the decision in the moment to take the bull by the horns. The greatest leaders confront change, and become the light when there is darkness. In regard to change, timing is everything.

Millennials are always hearing older generations tell stories about their "decades of experience." The truth is that circumstances look a lot different today than they did even five years ago. Change is constant, and sometimes decades of experience can blind a company's leadership. Looking backward won't always give you the answers you need to move forward. Experience is only useful if it's used to give a means of perspective for actions to be taken today and tomorrow. For example, the Pew Research Center found that only 12% of young adults used social media in 2005. Just ten years later, in 2015, the number of young adults using social media shot up to 90% (1). That statistic alone should give leaders insight to the actions they must take as our society becomes more technologically abundant.

The only thing in this world that *always* moves forward is time. Time only moves in one direction, and so should you. Moving back, looking back and stepping back will only give others the opportunity to step forward. Nostalgia is great on occasion, but don't be *that* person who's only living in the past.

I get it – taking that step forward takes bravery. Change isn't easy and that's why so few people do it. But all your fears will be eliminated once you take that step. All your inhibitions, all the little things in life that have stopped you – those things disappear when you step into the future. Companies will benefit from embracing and leveraging the changes that millennials seek. <u>In 21st century business, the seven most dangerous words are: "because that's how it's always been done."</u>

Right now, you have the opportunity to take the next step in life. Whether you're 18 or 85 doesn't matter; the next step is what will give you the vitality to live another day. Taking the next step will put a smile on your face. And taking the next step will help you create the change you've always dreamed of.

Perrin, A. (2015, October 08). Social Media Usage: 2005-2015. Retrieved November 05, 2016, from http://www.pewinter-net.org/2015/10/08/social-networking-usage-2005-2015/

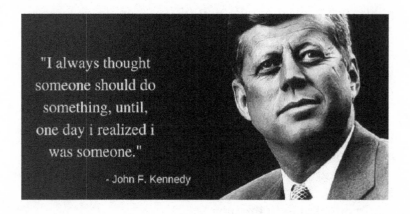

"I always thought someone should do something, until, one day i realized i was someone."

- John F. Kennedy

■ Differences

Contrary to popular belief, there are some similarities between millennials and our predecessors (I know, it's hard to believe). Millennials value having a successful marriage and being great parents (1). Personally, I can't see how any generation wouldn't value those things, but I've seen an increasing number of people who don't see themselves getting married and having kids. Since we value traveling and freedom, there's a segment of this generation that doesn't want what most Americans would consider a "traditional life." Although this isn't my line of thinking, I can empathize with the 21st century, free-spirited ideology.

Millennials, along with their elders, value helping others, especially those in need. I frequently tell others, "The most successful individuals are the ones who help the most people, no matter what your definition of success is!" People tend to think that's an oversimplification of a much more complicated issue, but it's not. Helping people will lead to a happy life full of relationships, money, fulfillment and opportunity. If you want to make a million dollars, start by helping a million people. <u>No matter how you define success, helping people is the common denominator</u>.

However, to completely empathize with the millennial generation, it's important to understand some of the key differentiating factors that have formed their new age ideology.

» Previous generations had a "leaning-back" type of attitude in the workplace, whereas millennials want to lean forward and engage in the experience. We want to participate! If you're not engaging a millennial, we're going to find an opportunity that's more enticing. This problem can be avoided by involving and allowing the millennial to participate in the decision-making process. <u>If you include millennials in the decision-making process, you're guaranteed to gain insight you would have never had otherwise</u>.

» Previous generations were typically cliquish and judgmental, whereas millennials are inclusive and tolerant (2). The more seats at the table, the more opportunity there is for collaboration. Keeping conversations between executives is short-sighted and risky. If you implement a change that negatively impacts customers (or employees), you're shooting yourself in the foot. Creating a collaborative culture where all perspectives are valued will make a millennial feel at home, and prevent decisions that negatively impact customers and employees. Millennials embrace diversity, and we live lives of inclusion and equality.

» Previous generations were anti-corporate, whereas millennials believe in commerce with conscience. Corporations have a responsibility today to do things ethically and in a way that benefits society, not just their bank accounts. The truth is, capitalism is evolving into an ideology that holds macro social, economic, and societal responsibility. Make your company more than just a profit and loss sheet – you're in business to make a positive impact on the world.

» Previous generations looked at parents as authority figures. Today, parents are friends and helpers. I hang out with my parents. They're cool, but in a completely nerdy way. I look to them for advice and they do the same to me. The tables are not uneven. Although they birthed me, my opinion means just as much as theirs. The authoritarian figures left the day I went to college. My parents are now people I confide in. Our relationship is now predicated on a friendship instead of a dictatorship.

» Previous generations had a period of their lives between dependence and independence that lasted a summer (between college and the real world). For millennials, this glory phase of life has been extended. We don't mind living with our parents and keeping our costs low. There was more pressure in the "good ol' days" to get out of your parents' house and create a life on your own. This has caused older generations to look at millennials as weak because we don't have the fortitude to live away from home. Is that true? Or do we just have a completely different set of values and social constructs that guide our lives today? Rest assured, as the millennial generation ages, the glory phase will end and we'll become normal consumers of household goods and services.

» Previous generations are considered "digital immigrants." Millennials are considered "digital natives." The way our brains are wired is completely different (for better or for worse). Although research in brain development among millennials is new, some medical experts say that the brains of people in this generation are physically developing differently because of their almost constant interaction with technology (3). Older generations had to learn technology after their formative years, whereas technology is ingrained in a millennials DNA. Think about how much screen time a baby boomer had from the ages of 0-18 compared to a millennial. Our brains are evolving, and so are the ways we communicate and systematize activities in our day to day lives.

» Previous generations were led by mass media. Today, personal (or social) media reigns supreme. The opinions of influencers now travel far and wide across the world in a matter of seconds. The largest media company in the world (Facebook) doesn't produce any media; it's all user generated. This is giving people a voice and corruption an antagonist. Whether you do something good or bad, social media is bound to magnify your actions. Harmful actions are no longer swept under the rug because of modern media practices. Social Media is a digital footprint that holds people accountable

Boomers, you had the shooting of JFK and drug addicts. We have 9/11 and social media addicts. You can sit there and complain about how "different" millennials are, or you can use their perspective to make better decisions moving forward. The choice is yours.

These differences may seem miniscule, but they shaped us throughout our formative years. Millennials are no better or worse than any other generation before us. In conversations with elders I've found that every generation has expressed defiance toward the social norms that were imposed on them.

As times continue to change, millennials get more and more heat from older generations. James Franco once famously said that "They hate us cause they ain't us," but that's not the case here. The reality is that we're different, just like every generation that came before us. I think there's a sense of jealousy that's manifested into dislike, one formed from the idea that millennials have had everything handed to them, and that they have an abundance of opportunities surrounding them. Perhaps there's even a sense of jealousy that millennials have had it a little easier than other generations did during our childhood. Previous generations should be proud that they have been able to provide millennials with unprecedented opportunities. We thank you.

Boomers, when you were in high school, the main question you had was, "Where are all my friends and what are they doing?" And that's awesome! There was a very short phase of my life where I had the same question.

However, in the age of technology, that question is one social media post away from an answer. People in my generation are asking questions like, "How do I connect with more people like me? Or different than me?" Or maybe a question like, "How can I share more information to attract the talent, conversations, and customers that will help me grow and thrive for years to come?" Those questions were a lot harder to answer, "back in the day," but today, they're extremely applicable. Future generations may be asking completely different questions, and that's a good thing. The questions we're asking show how our society has advanced over time. Again, this doesn't make us better or worse than any other generation; just different.

As hard as this may be to believe, millennials are the new hot thing today. Eventually, we won't be.

Eventually, Generation Z will be the cool trendsetters and millennials will be giving today's youngsters flack on how "they have it easy." Technology has made all our lives easier, but it's also caused problems we couldn't fathom a decade ago. The truth is that every generation is supposed to be making it a little easier for the generation that follows them. That's social evolution. That's the progression of life.

The Millennial Generation Research Review. (2016, September 02). Retrieved November 05, 2016, from https://www.us-chamberfoundation.org/reports/millennial-generation-research-review

T. (2011, June 10). TEDxSF Scott Hess Millennials: Who They Are & Why We Hate Them. Retrieved November 05, 2016, from https://www.youtube.com/watch?v=P-enHH-r FM

Technology is changing the Millennial brain. (n.d.). Retrieved November 05, 2016, from http://publicsource.org/investi-gations/technology-changing-millennial-brain#.WG0gX-rYrLL9

History

I f millennials aren't a part of your history, they will be in the near future. History is one of those things that *everyone* loves to talk about. Every day, every person on this planet can make history. Every day is a canvas waiting to be painted, or a movie waiting to be shot. You're the main character and the producer. You get to choose the supporting cast, the setting, and the actions that take place. All the moments in your life are a part of your history.

At the end of your life, this movie you directed (or this picture you painted) will either serve as a warning or an example. To give you a frame of reference: Hitler's life was a warning, and Nelson Mandela's life was an example. Everyone reading this book is looking to set an example for future generations, and pave a road for innovation and growth.

Every day we live, we leave a legacy. For many people, their only legacy is their digital footprint. All of us hope that millennials see past their digital presence and look to create impact offline. What we've done online is great, but it's ever-evolving. We don't hear many people today talking about AOL or Myspace unless it's the butt of a joke. We need to look to create a legacy that extends further than what our search history says about us.

If we want to create history, we must craft our own vision for the future. We must know exactly what we want and visualize it. <u>Before anyone else can see it or believe it, you must see it and believe it yourself</u>.

People get caught up in their past and focus on what's not possible because of what once was. However, history is created by looking forward not backward. We can't do anything about what happened yesterday, or what will happen tomorrow. But, we all have full control over what's happening right now. Our elders tend to look backward because their successes may be behind them. Millennials tend to look forward because that's where our future successes lie. One way of thinking isn't necessarily better than the other, but most would agree that it's best to focus on what we have full control over: the present moment. Experience is only valuable if it continues to grow our foresight and ability to take action. Once we create a vision and an outcome for our future, all we need to do is reverse engineer that outcome so we can take the first step. Visions aren't attained overnight; they're attained by taking one step at a time.

Many of my connections have plans to make history, and I fully support them. During our discussions, I make sure to reiterate that their vision may take 1,000 steps. But, the only thing they need to figure out is the first step. We must stop getting caught up on all the little steps in the middle. <u>History is made by taking the next step</u>. Step one leads to step two. The people who never make history are the ones who complain about all the work it'll take to reach step 1,000. The people who end up making history don't know every step they must take. They use "just in time learning" to personalize their education for where and when they need it (1). If we're self-aware of the next step in front of us, we can accomplish *anything.*

Our lives, everything we want, need, and desire, are based around human emotion. We want to find as many of the good emotions as possible and get rid of the bad. All emotions, both good and bad, are created through an experience. If we want to create a positive experience and enhance history, we need to always have something in life to look forward to. Without that feeling of anticipation, our life fizzles down to previous experiences. Our personal histories are just filled with emotions and fleeting moments which are instantly replaced by the next experience.

Complacent and comfortable people rarely have things to look forward to. They are stuck in the same patterns and habits day after day after day, and for some people, that's good. But the things we look forward to in life are the events on our calendar that break our patterns. These are the moments that are just a little different than what we experience in our everyday lives. If we don't have anything in life to look forward to, then what's the point?

History isn't about creating a life for others to read about. History is about living every moment to its fullest, and making a difference in the lives of those you surround yourself with. It's about experiencing all the joys that life has to offer, and trying new things that can open up a new world of opportunity. Millennials are looking to experience this through the work they do and the products they consume. They want to accomplish the "unattainable" and make sure they create incredible experiences for themselves and others along the way.

So, whatever it is that you've been thinking about accomplishing – just do it. Make the decision to take control of your destiny. We only have one life and there are too many mediocre things in this world to end your life saying things like: I wish, I could, I almost and I didn't. We want to say things like: I did, I'm glad, I tried, I failed and I succeeded. Those are the moments we want to cherish throughout life. All successes start with someone's vision to make history.

No matter who you are or where you came from, you can become successful and you can make history. Success is a choice. Making history and changing the world are also choices. You can do, be, love and create anything you want in this world.

This is not a belief synonymous with millennials, rather, this is a reality of modern day life. Millennials believe that, in the 21st century, anyone can make a difference if they take the right steps. Every day is a blessing and every day you have a chance to make history. Your own history. And maybe, if you're lucky, it'll affect someone else's.

You can sit there and watch history, or you can go and create it. The choice is yours.

Hatcher, A. (2015, January 16). 5 Reasons Just-in-Time Learning Rocks. Retrieved November 05, 2016, from http://lpd.nau.edu/5-reasons-just-time-learning-rocks/

■ The Early Years

Self-awareness about our past is what helps us create history moving forward. Just like every other generation, events from our formative years continue to shape our perspective on society.

Besides Columbine, the first life-altering global event that happened during our childhood was undoubtedly September 11, 2001. This experience flooded our brains with fear. Is the world a safe place? Is terrorism something we'll have to face our whole lifetime? Why would someone do this to us? These are all questions that go through a child's mind when an event like 9/11 occurs. Our generation has grown up with terrorism as part of our lives. Many of us look at the world as a more fearful place because of these events.

This experience also brought upon it political implications that lead to distrust. We started a war (Iraq) based on false information, and paid for it with credit that didn't exist (thanks China). How are we supposed to trust a public sector that manipulates things for financial and political gain?

Another impactful event was the pop of the housing bubble that caused the recession in 2008. We watched rich people become poor and poor people become rich. The housing market and mortgage industry put the American economy in a tail spin. But above all, our society faltered because of a <u>culture of consumerism</u>.

People were spending money they didn't have on things they didn't need.

Millennials recognized the poor purchasing habits of our elders and realized that this event was completely avoidable. Why do we need to buy houses, fancy cars and jewelry that we don't need? We don't! This has led many millennials to value experiences over goods. That nice shiny object we spent $5,000 on isn't so shiny in two months. The experiences and adventures we create will stay shiny in our memory for the rest of our lives.

That fact alone will have global economic implications as American consumerism has and will continue to, "trim the fat." Companies will start to lose market share's if they don't provide emotionally satisfying experiences based on a foundation of social values. Because of this, millennials look to buy things they need, based on brands they trust, from people they respect. We realize that our environment (and society as a whole) is something that must be preserved and cherished. We tend to get frustrated when sustainability gets thrown out the window for more wasteful, and divisive alternatives.

Many brick and mortar stores have lost the battle to the e-commerce revolution. If we want a product, it can be delivered to our door the following day. Millennials tend to prefer the instant gratification that the internet has provided us.

Remember CD players, camcorders, digital cameras, PDA's, MP3 players and GPS systems? Those don't even exist anymore. We saw the invention of the smartphone wipe out entire industries. Do you have a problem that needs fixing? Are you looking to save time on the most menial tasks? There's probably an app for that.

The instant gratification culture has both driven our society forward and held us back. There are people with social media addictions, psychological disorders, insomnia and FOMO (fear of missing out) because of the technological advances that have shaped our generation.

We've been shaped by natural disasters, political drama, tech bubbles and most of all, media. For the first time ever, personal media is just as large as (if not larger than) mass media. We've grown up in a society where every day something else is going "viral." There are so many different touch points today that we've become desensitized to death, criminality and damage or destruction of any kind. The normalization of terrible events every day across the world is creating a society of people who lack empathy and sympathy (1). Unfortunately, it feels like we've become numb to the over saturation of both pain and pleasure due to social media.

The death of Myspace and the birth of Facebook brought about change we couldn't fathom at the time. People have become more interested in what's going on in the world of social media than what's going on in the world around them. We've become so connected with the world around us that we've become exponentially disconnected with ourselves. Many of us no longer live in the present moment. Our society will continue to teeter back and forth between social media as a valuable resource, and social media as an inhibiting obsession. There's no doubt that social media-centered services will be a part of this generation and our society for decades to come. It's time to learn how to productively use these tools, or suffer from the addiction many people face on a daily basis.

Boase, M. (n.d.). The Social and Emotional Impact of 'Everywhere' Technology – Lambda Mi Education and Development. Retrieved November 05, 2016, from http://www.lambda-mi.com/the-social-and-emotional-impact-of-everywhere-technology/

■ Engaging and Empowering

I f we're not empowering, we're disempowering. If we're not engaged, we're disengaged. If we're not moving forward, we're getting left behind. When it comes to the fork in the road, millennials only see one path. We are all looking to be engaged and empowered both in our personal and professional lives.

The experiences we have throughout our lives either help us grow or help us die. However, sometimes we forget that death is simply the absence of life. This holds true for many things in our world:

» Failure is the absence of success.

» Cold is the absence of heat (1).

» Pain is the absence of pleasure.

» Darkness is the absence of light.

» Ignorance is the absence of intelligence.

» Corruption is the absence of integrity.

» Scarcity is the absence of abundance.

And decay is the absence of growth. If employees are not engaged and empowered they could be a cancer to your organization. Gallup estimates that actively disengaged employees cost the U.S. $450 to $550 billion in lost productivity each year (2). This type of disconnect goes viral in organizations because actively disengaged employees can encourage others on their team to disengage as well. One disengaged person on one team can bring down a whole company.

As employers, we seek to remove disengagement and promote a productive and healthy working environment. Productivity is something that's cherished, but not often found. We are flooded with the TV, Internet, and a million other distractions and data points in this world. Very few things in society help us grow and attain the things we desire most in our lives. If management creates a workplace that engages someone to their core, they'll have the opportunity to help their teams tap into their peak performance. This is every manager's fantasy. If you dream of an engaged workplace, it's time to stop thinking and start doing.

The key to growth is momentum, and momentum starts with taking the first step. The best teams get addicted to the momentum that creates an engaging and empowering work place. In the following chapters, I'll show you how to engineer your personal momentum.

The whole concept behind this book is how to engage and empower a millennial. Empathy is becoming less and less common within our society, but it's one of the most important skills when operating in a multi-generational workforce. We know that for companies to progressively grow their team, they need to do the following:

» Create a flexible work environment

» Create a culture of collaboration and teamwork

» Leverage technology

» Provide quality training and upward mobility

» Always be looking to improve systems and policies

» Be willing to have open conversations, even if they're uncomfortable

» Understand the human emotions that drive us forward and hold us back

This list of growth activities could go on forever. However, to obtain corporate growth, organizations must concentrate on the development of their people. For people to grow, they need to become self-aware, and self-awareness starts with our mind and body.

Mind

Our mind is the most powerful operating system (software) on the planet. It runs from the day we're born until the day we die, and very few people take the time to fully develop its capabilities. The battle between the "good guy" and the "bad guy" who sit over our shoulders is something that everyone must deal with. Our mind is driven by emotion. Our minds determine what we're going to focus on and what we inevitably attract. Our minds have the power to change our own lives and those we surround ourselves with. The power of the mind is determined by the willfulness of its owner to explore it.

Body

Our body is the most powerful machine (hardware) on the planet. Becoming mindful of our body is easy because we can see it, unlike the inner confines of our brain. Compare an empowered person and a lazy person. What's the difference? Are they breathing deep? Is their chin up? Are they smiling? Are their shoulders back or are they slouched? Are they excited or dismal? Most people intuitively understand the physiology of an engaged and empowered individual.

Although I believe that complete alignment involves the mind, body, and spirit, I have left "spirit" out of this conversation because it's an individual journey.

Companies should respect the fact that everyone has a different view on what the human spirit (and spirituality) means to them. I share my views on this topic at toward the end of this book.

When I'm working with organizations in peak performance workshops, I focus on helping people create their success identity and what I would consider "the best versions of themselves." We all have a best version of ourselves and what defines that version is a certain pattern. When we're unstoppable, our mind and our body are in a certain pattern. We have a sense of *congruency*, and we're moving forward in a specific direction.

But on the flip side, if we're the worst version of ourselves (depressed, frustrated, upset, pissed off, etc.), we're also in a certain pattern. Emotional states are created by the patterns within our mind and body. Happiness is a pattern and so is depression. So, when we're trying to understand how to engage a millennial, we're really looking to understand what patterns and emotional states we need to leverage to develop them into leaders.

Within a company, the main job of leadership is to get employees to their peak performance capabilities. It's the most important scope of work of any manager. They must engage their employees at a level that produces massive results – ones far greater than expected.

The success of any company, community or country is based off the ebb and flow of emotion. The emotional states of your followers determine their engagement or lack thereof. If a company is looking to properly grow their millennial workforce, understanding who they are and what they want will allow the organization to create a multi-generational powerhouse.

Anjara, A. (2015, July 11). Cold Is Absence of Heat And Nothing More. Retrieved November 05, 2016, from http://www.geek-pause.com/brain-teasers/cold-is-absence-of-heat/

Gallup. (2013, June 11). How to Tackle U.S. Employees' Stagnating Engagement. Retrieved January, 2017, from http://www.gallup.com/businessjournal/162953/tackl e-employ-ees-stagnating-engagement.aspx

■ Life Experiences

L ife is no longer about working to make money just so that we can pay taxes and spend what's left. In other words, millennials don't want to live to work; they want to work to live. This generation is always looking for that special experience.

Three in 4 millennials (78%) would choose to spend money on a desirable experience or event over purchasing an item (1).

Life is about experiencing what the world has to offer. Why work for 40 years doing something that's only "okay"? There are too many mediocre things in this world to spend almost half our lives doing work that's only "okay."

Why be okay when you can be awesome? Why live a good life when you can live a great life? I know that I'm oversimplifying something that's a bit more complicated. But, let's call it what it is: living an awesome life is a choice. We all have the opportunity to make that decision.

When millennials think of living an awesome life, they're looking for experiences that put a smile on their faces. They want joy, adventure, excitement, happiness, thrill and surprises. You'll notice that each of these are emotions that can be obtained without money. Can money help create these emotions? Yup, but it's not a necessity.

The main way our generation gets life experiences is through travel. Whether it's for business or pleasure, domestic or international, it doesn't really matter. The fact that we get to experience something new and different satisfies some of those desirable emotions that give our life vitality. Many millennials have the desire to go to every continent, something that wasn't valued as highly in previous generations.

The need for life experiences stretches far beyond an airplane. If a millennial is shopping at a mall, they want to be immersed in an experiential retail environment. It's the experience of shopping that gets us out of the house. If you're not providing an experience, they might as well just go on Amazon, purchase the same product and get two-day shipping. If they're leaving the house, they're looking for a moment that will put a smile on their face.

If they're going out to eat, they're looking for something exotic and adventurous. Some of my favorite meals have been from a food truck on the curb of a street. The tastes. The sounds. The hustle and bustle of people. It's fun. It's entertaining. And, it's a moment that I won't ever forget. We're always looking for new dining experiences – something awesome to tell our friends about.

Even if you're managing a millennial, look for a way to give them an experience that they can take with them for the rest of their lives. Give them a magical moment that they'll want to tell their friends and family about. If you're lucky, they'll make a social media post about what you (or your company) did for them.

So, be spontaneous. Be the light. Be the type of person that creates magic. We've all heard how it's been done for the last 100 years. That's boring. Show them something new. Show them something different or something that will knock their socks off.

If you're looking to retain millennials as employees, this is especially important. I've worked with too many sales people that are in the 9 to 5 p.m., Monday to Friday grind. "I have numbers to hit this week, and the same numbers to hit next week." BORING!

I understand that business is about making money. But what about sharing stories? What about innovative training? What about games during lunch? What about creating magical moments and experiences? What about a bar tab for happy hour on a Friday? Do something different. Eventually people hit a breaking point where "the same old, same old" needs a software update. If a millennial is looking for an upgrade, then it probably doesn't involve your company.

The millennial generation is looking for experiences that get them excited. They are looking to get involved in things like:

» Travel

» Money management

» Spontaneity

» Philanthropy

» Creative activities

» Hobbies

» Exercise

» Family time

» Learning something new

» FUN!

» Innovative technology that creates an experience

» Helping peers attain an outcome

» Reflection and meditation

» Spending time outdoors

» Mastering a specific action

» Eating awesome food

Millennials are motivated by activities that are emotionally satisfying. They want to experience what the world has to offer, and help their peers do the same. New experiences bring about new perspectives, which provide a world of opportunity.

Managers should look at lists like these and think of ways they can create experiences for their millennial counterparts. <u>All companies are really in the business of creating magical moments</u>. If you do that for us, we'll give you the world in return.

<u>Millennials Fueling The Experience Economy. (2014).</u> *<u>Retrieved November 05, 2016, from</u>* *<u>https://eventbrites3.s3.amazonaws.com/marketing/Mil lennials_Research/Gen_PR_Final.pdf</u>*

■ Vision

When people align their identity with their intentions, a vision is created. So often in life we get stuck in the day to day grind and lose sight of the bigger picture – *why*? If we want to achieve something, we need to have the vision when we begin that our outcome *can* and *will* happen. The trick is to have the long-term vision while focusing on the next step in front of us. It's an art.

Millennials dream big. They have some hefty goals on things they want to accomplish before they leave this planet. Many people of older generations would refer to some of these visions as hallucinations. Often, elders tell us that what we want just isn't possible. If you're looking to work with a millennial, it's important to stop telling them that their vision will never come to fruition. Show us the light, not the darkness. Show us the journey and the destination. But realize that nothing great ever happened from talking about what isn't possible.

It's important that as we go through this merging of the minds, that we come from a place of understanding each other. Millennials need to understand the visions of other generations, and vice versa.

Here's the vision most millennials have for a better future:

» Violence is mitigated and hopefully abolished. The fact that our society is concerned about getting shot in public places is absolutely insane. This transformation involves change in gun laws, which is tied to a larger mental health issue, which is tied to police brutality, which is tied to our justice system. Our government and media perpetuate fear and violence. Unfortunately, fixing an issue like this is bigger than just a gun law. An ideal society is filled with more love than violence. Millennials are working every day to rid our society of violence and ignorance.

» Equality – not just the type we talk about in fairy tales and social media posts.

» A clean planet. Our oceans, our cities and our suburbs have trash, everywhere. Some places are cleaner than others, but our society doesn't currently put precedence on preserving our planet and its resources. Today, we are abusing our environment like an addict would a drug. We must invest in the global ecosystem to make sure it thrives for years to come.

» Education that has real world application. We'll discuss this more in future chapters.

» Politics that are decentralized from the party system. There's a legitimate separation of church and state – not just one we talk about. There's transparency from our government. People's voices are actually heard, not oppressed by the political system that only serves private interest and party lines.

» Organized religion is not a part of everyday life yet human spirituality and connection is at an all-time high. The concept of "what was taught to you, is not always good for you" is implemented throughout our society. People develop their own belief system structured around exactly what works for them. This creates a great environment for individual enlightenment, which naturally get dismissed in the presence of traditional religious citations. Humanity becomes more accepting of others who have different belief systems.

» Going to work is something that we want to do, not something that we have to do. People will empower themselves to find a positive working environment that allows them to grow and thrive.

» America has found the happy medium between being "the world leader" and "sticking our nose in everyone's business." We're no longer fighting other people's wars, but are there to support communities we align with. This is a complicated issue and one that won't be solved until our political system is straightened out.

» We provide housing and food for the homeless and less fortunate. This will lower healthcare costs for taxpayers, and clear out emergency rooms so we can get service when we need it. It will free up our jails and allow our police force to protect us from "the real bad guys." Providing food and housing for those who need it is creating a tangible foundation for America (1).

Is this vision optimistic and idealistic? Of course, it is. But, every great feat started with a vision to attain it. Elders may think this list sounds delusional, but millennials will do everything in our power to turn this world into a modern masterpiece. Do some of these things already exist? Of course, but not to the extent that they should.

Everyone needs to envision exactly what they want their world to be like and go create it. Within every organization (and personal journey) there needs to be a leader who is constantly reiterating the vision, no matter how tough the going gets. There are too many people who have a vision, but wait for others to go make it happen. We must see the change. Plan the change. Then, *be* the change. It'll all be worth it.

Schiller, B. (2014, April 01). Housing The Homeless Saves Money Here's The Research That Proves It. Retrieved November 07, 2016, from http://www.fastcoexist.com/3028384/housing-the-homeless-saves-money-heres-the-research-that-proves-it

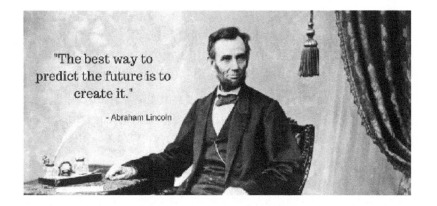

"The best way to predict the future is to create it."

- Abraham Lincoln

■ Purpose

I f you haven't discovered your purpose yet, it's time to take a good, hard look at your personal *why* and *how* you're moving towards it. This is one of the most important questions you will ever answer. Millennials tend to be very introspective and purpose driven.

People spend their whole lives in the pursuit of their purpose. If you don't have a purpose, you could be missing a sense of fulfillment that money can't buy.

Achieving results and goals are easy; there's a science to it. If we want to make a certain amount of money, we can follow a hypothetical set of 10 steps. If we want to travel the world on less than $15,000, that's easy, we can follow a travel bloggers 10 steps. It seems like there's a 10-step system to achieving anything we set our mind to.

However, there's no 10-step system for feeling fulfilled at the end of the day. What makes you feel fulfilled and what makes me feel fulfilled may be completely different. Tony Robbins always told me that the art of fulfillment is something very few people master.

If we want to feel fulfilled, we need to know what's really driving us forward. What makes us want to wake up in the morning? What makes us want to achieve the things we want in our lives? Who do we need to become in order to die a happy person? <u>Writing down simple things like, who we are, what we do, what we want and</u>

<u>where we're going can allow us to slowly uncover this complicated issue</u>.

Millennials tend to be purpose driven and not paycheck driven. We want to feel like we're making a difference in this world every day we wake up. The best way to make a difference is to help people in need. If your business happens to solve the specific problem a group of people have, then you're on the right track.

Companies like Ultimate Software allow employees to work on passion projects during work hours (1). This generation wants to complete meaningful work that creates impact. Contrary to investor's beliefs, impact does not always have a direct dollar figure. Millennials are happiest and most engaged when they feel they are doing meaningful work. Happy employees make happy customers. Happy customers spend more money. And all of that translates to increased revenue, productivity, and most of all, fulfillment in the workplace. The success of every company lies on the shoulders of happy and engaged employees.

Creating a purposeful work experience is one of the most important retention strategies a company has. And, if your company is not creating a workplace experience with purpose, the easiest way to change it is to ask your employees what *you* can do better. It's really that simple.

If you're a helpless manager wondering how to uncover your employee's mojo, you're in the right spot. Helping others discover their purpose can be an enlightening experience in itself. A recent Gallup study found that millennials, more so than any other generation before them, are asking themselves, "Does this organization value my strengths and my contribution (2)?" No one in this generation cares about fixing our weaknesses.

We want to maximize our strengths. Why focus on something we're bad at? Managers should be using a strengths-based approach to customize millennials scope of work regardless of their job title. Playing to the strengths of your people will *always* be a winning strategy.

If a company wants to play to the strengths of their team, they must make sure they're in the constant pursuit of development. Job satisfaction is important, but personal satisfaction reigns supreme. If we feel like we're growing mentally, physically and emotionally on a daily basis, we feel fulfilled. We'll come to work invigorated, ready to help make a difference every day.

There's no better time than now to understand your purpose and have an open conversation with your team about what they're really going after in life. Teams driven by a common ideology are stronger and more cohesive than those who have scattered visions. Besides getting to know the group a little better, you may discover that you have more in common with your team than you originally thought.

Attracting and Retaining Millennials in the Global Workplace. (2016, June 24). Retrieved November 07, 2016, from http://www.aperianglobal.com/attracting-retaining-millenni-als-global-workplace/

Gallup, I. (2016, May 11). Millennials: How They Live and Work. Retrieved November 07, 2016, from http://www.gallup.com/opinion/chairman/191426/millennials-live-work.aspx

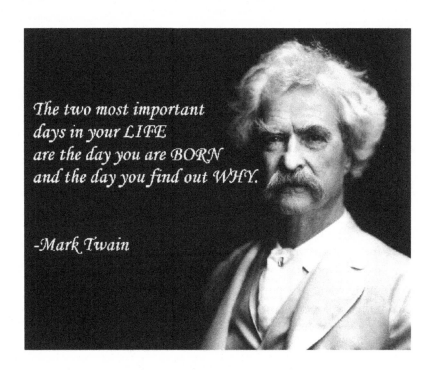

The two most important
days in your LIFE
are the day you are BORN
and the day you find out WHY.

-Mark Twain

◼ Personal Brand

n order to understand how millennials look to brand themselves, you need to fully grasp the concept of individualism. When people ask me to describe my generation in one word, I answer with, "individualism." We aren't one of seven billion. We are one of one. We tend to judge all generations based on a collective ideology. However, we must recognize that generations are made up of individuals and millennials embrace that individualistic perspective.

It's always interested me how millennials are so team oriented and inclusive, yet have a strong sense of individualism that drives them forward. Although millennials want to be a part of the bigger picture, they're very concerned with their personal interests being a part of that picture. At times, these desires are projected onto social media for everyone to see.

There will always be those who post selfies of themselves in the bathroom, and boomerangs with kissy faces. I have nothing particularly positive to say about those actions. What I will say is that some influencers use their sense of individualism to help their followers. Others, not so much. Gerard Adams, founder of Elite Daily, always says "leaders create leaders." I couldn't agree more.

Today's influencers have turned their individuality into what some would call a religion. They share their beliefs and teachings to their social followings (both in person and digitally). Followers end up taking little bits and pieces from other ideologies to develop their own. I've personally adopted many perspectives from Steve Jobs, Tony Robbins, Oren Klaff, Grant Cardone, Marc Cuban and even people like Albert Einstein, Nelson Mandela, Henry Ford and Nicola Tesla.

With these ideologies, I have created my own mojo and formed my own message. This is my sense of individualism. Today I impose some of my beliefs on my followers, and that's a good thing. I don't expect every person to adopt every one of my beliefs. What I expect is that others look at my ideology, put it up against their own, and then decide which constructs they would like to add to (or eliminate from) their life. Many of my thoughts are meant to be sounding boards for others to create their own philosophies. The best way for us to grow our perspective is to seek to understand other viewpoints. It's this understanding that allows us to adopt new, empowering beliefs.

Contrary to some beliefs, our high sense of individualism does not limit our overall collectivism. Millennials tend to be more caring, community oriented and politically engaged than previous generations (1). We want to be a part of a team that's driven toward a purpose, but have the ability to bring our sense of individualism to the table for the greater good of the group. If everyone has the same perspective, the concept of collectivism is almost null and void. Just because we want to choose our own path forward doesn't mean we can't rally for the greater good of the team.

The way millennials think is completely different than any generation before us. The principles of organized politics and religion have been (and will continue to be) fragmented and diluted to create more modern, decentralized ideologies. These new principles will be reconstructed and brought to light by those with the highest sense of individualism.

When people endorse something, they inevitably make it part of their "personal brand." This goes for politics and religion, as well as the products people use. Tattoos themselves are the most literal form of the word "brand." We are defined not only by what we do and use, but by who we are and the choices we make. Every decision we make is a piece of our personal brand. Every social media post we create is a representation of who we are and what we stand for.

I believe that people will start carefully choosing the brands they use and endorse, as well as the posts they make. It's my hope that people will start filtering out the noise and hiding their own ignorance. Everyone has seen a friend publicize their stupidity with their online actions.

The movement toward personal branding has done wonders for the spread of ideas. The rise of technology has provided a platform for both diplomatic and offensive ideologies. <u>Regardless if we agree with another's perspective, political correctness is the largest form of mental oppression</u>. Social constructs from our past create today's ideologies that we use to drive our lives forward. <u>However, if we never challenge the traditions from our past, how are we supposed to advance and grow as a society</u>? The millennial philosophy throws political correctness out the window for the greater good of humanity. Today, people speak their minds, and that's doing wonders for some of the more uncomfortable conversations we face in society today.

People tend to avoid uncomfortable conversations because it's offensive. You want to live in a democracy, but you don't want to be offended? That seems a bit counterintuitive. If you're offended by someone's words or actions, it's subjective, and has everything to do with you as an individual (and the meaning you attach to that specific action).

Frankly, the personal branding movement is uncovering all the assholes in the world. It used to be that assholes were just assholes inside their own homes. Now, they share their "asshole" ideology with the rest of the world in order to herd in more assholes. There are assholes in every generation. Personal branding has allowed assholes to show their true colors.

Personal branding makes it easier for employers to fire (or hire) the people they see aligning with certain ideologies. Are employees endorsing a certain movement that makes your company look bad? Are they making shrewd comments that make your company look trashy? Are they creating content that doesn't align with the philosophies of the organization? Show them the front door, and next time, be a little more conscientious during the hiring process.

There's no shame in making a bad hiring decision, or letting go of an unruly customer. But, with today's big data, it's now easier than ever to choose which people align with your company's brand identity.

The Millennial Generation Research Review. (2016, September02). Retrieved September 22, 2016, from https://www.us-chamberfoundation.org/reports/millennial-generation-re-search-review

◼ Power of Influence

If you search the top 20 brands, 25% of the search results will end up being user generated content. And guess who's producing that content? You guessed it millennials (1). They're producing content that's influencing purchasing decisions of people across the world.

When a baby boomer wants to make a purchasing decision, they turn to us. We're in tune with what's happening today. We know where to look for reviews, and most likely have acquaintances who use similar products. Millennials want to keep their parents and others in our society on trend.

We're not only influencing purchasing decisions, but also the workplace. Millennials will account for seventy-five percent of the total global workforce by 2025 (2). Consumers and employees are steadily adopting the millennial ideology, regardless of their age. Seventy-five percent of the workforce is not an employment democracy, it's an oligarchy.

This will inevitably cause a culture shift across every industry. Fortunately, there are many businesses adapting their workplace to the changing times. However, there are others lagging behind, and if those organizations don't make the proper shift, they will lose to their competitors who do.

Consumers now educate themselves before making a purchasing decision. Our choices are based on research from what we find online. We read reviews, test out products, talk with friends and return items we don't like. Millennial influence is on the rise, and many corporations are shaking in their boots. A few bad reviews on Yelp or Amazon and your product could get a bad rap. Change in the purchasing process has caused companies to innovate not only products, but also customer service. The first point of contact during a mishap with a product is a company's customer service rep, and millennials expect that person on the other end of the call to interact like a human, not a robot.

Millennials are driving reviews, user created content and social media transparency, and no business has the power to stop it. This is what a movement is all about. It's the transferring of power, influence and eventually, money. The largest generation of all time has the power to determine the fate of your business or organization. Tread carefully, or experience the silence of failure.

Millennials: Defined, Explained & Illustrated. (2014, July 08). Retrieved November 07, 2016, from https://www.youtube.com/watch?v=bt8cfeBM4mI

The Millennial Generation Research Review. (2016, September02). Retrieved November 05, 2016, from https://www.us-chamberfoundation.org/reports/millennial-generation-research-review

What We Believe

■ Equality

Millennials are the first generation to grow up with equality as an expectation, not an exception. Equality throughout our history has evolved through some of America's greatest leaders. One of the first American heroes to stand up for equality was Abraham Lincoln who signed the Emancipation Proclamation. In the 1960s, Martin Luther King catalyzed the steady decline of racism that had been experienced throughout history. Although inequality is still a modern reality, our society is beginning to realize that everyone deserves an equal opportunity.

Today, gay people can legally get married, which set new precedence for LGBTQ+ rights. Barack Obama became the first black president, and, for better or for worse, we have longtime entrepreneur Donald Trump to shake up the Washington establishment. Never before has our country set precedence like this. And yet still, millennials rate social and economic inequality as the top challenge the world faces globally and locally (1). It's obvious that we have a bumpy road ahead of us, but we have come a long way.

Whether you're gay, straight, black, white, male, female, Christian or Jewish you have the right to become as successful as you want to be. You can do, be, become, create, build and achieve anything you set your mind to. If someone else has done it, so can you. Success is a choice, and every American can choose to be successful.

All you have to do is put in the work and travel the path to success one step at a time. Anyone can make that decision.

In 1776, the founding fathers of America wrote about "life, liberty and the pursuit of happiness." Anyone can become successful today if they really want to. The only things holding them back are the excuses they keep telling themselves.

Race, gender and sexuality no longer define the ability for someone to become successful. We live in a society with blurred gender roles and a support system for every cause. We are defined today by what we do, not by the boxes we check on a form.

Equality is in.

It's new. It's hip. It's happenin'. And it's here to stay.

But, as equal as we've become in some areas, we've regressed in others.

The digital world has created a whole new platform for the expression of inequality. If you don't believe it, try having a conversation with someone who fights for human rights, anticorruption, and against gun violence and climate change. The internet has become a very frustrating place to hang out for those intolerant of ignorance.

With the spread of smartphones, we're now seeing some of the worst police brutality to ever be recorded. As a society, we are now realizing that many of our country's inadequacies have been swept under the rug for decades; police brutality is just one example.

Smart phones and social media have given us a platform to address the serious mental health problem in this country (and around the world). Our police force, and society as a whole, often mistake felons for people who aren't properly medicated. Nationwide, people with mental health conditions constitute 64% of the jail population, according to the Federal Bureau of Prison Statistics (2). Statistics like this further perpetuate the economic inequality that millennials fight for.

Today, we overlook the terrorism and police shootings as something that's simply a part of our society. Our world has become numb to this type of violence and it's time for change. Millennials are so used to these types of news stories; but we need to stop and ask ourselves, "Are these events really the price of freedom?"

Don't get it twisted. Ninety-nine percent of cops are great. Ninety-nine percent of Muslims aren't terrorists. And ninety-nine percent of Americans aren't trying to kill you. But there is a 1% out there that's instilling our world with fear – and fear has been (and always will be) the easiest way to manipulate people. Companies and politicians have been using fear mongering for centuries.

The only reason people in this world hate is because they were taught to do it. People are taught to hate by other ignorant people who may not have known any better. No one on this earth was born a bigot. If bigotry can be learned, then it can also be unlearned.

The truth is that we aren't one of five races. We aren't one of five religions. We aren't one of two political parties. We are all one race – the human race. The more time we spend separating ourselves, the less time we spend working together to change this world for the better.

We can't succumb to the pressure of separating ourselves from each other. Political parties and religions are convenient ways to separate you from me. They don't bring the majority of us together, they spread us apart. The only purpose of categorization is to show someone how we are right and they are wrong. Categorizing individuals by their race, gender or sexual orientation is only bringing up the darkness from our past. Instead of looking for differences between each other, we should be actively engaging in conversations to find middle grounds. Unfortunately, we happen to live in a world that highlights differences and polarity over similarities.

Discrimination against younger generations because of differences only brings about a negative reflection of the antagonist. The reality is, there will always be bigotry in this world; it's impossible to eradicate all ideological differences. But, in a society where fear and anger can be found everywhere, love and community will always prevail.

"When the <u>power of love</u> overcomes the <u>love of power</u>, the world will know peace." Jimi Hendrix

Cann, O. (2015, October 25). Millennials Rate Social and Economic Inequality as Top Challenge Globally and Locally. Retrieved November 11, 2016, from <u>https://www.weforum.org/press/2015/10/millennials -rate-social-and-economic-inequality-as-top-challenge-globally-and-locally/</u>

Published by the World Economic Forum Impact of Disproportionate Incarceration of and Violence Against Black People with Mental Health Conditions In the World's Largest Jail System. (2014, August). Retrieved November 11, 2016, from <u>http://tbinternet.ohchr.org/Treaties/CERD/Shared%20 Documents/USA/INT CERD NGO USA 17740 E.pdf</u>

■ Education

As the most "educated" generation ever (1), millennials tend to look at our education system quite differently than others. Education is a concept that's been fought over for centuries. American society has welcomed major innovations in seemingly every industry *except* education. Although education has become gender equal, we're still using a system that was built during the Industrial Age. There have been a few changes, but most would argue that our youth are not better equipped than their international competition. When it comes to education, America is still trying to figure it out.

Some would argue that most of what's taught in school isn't relevant in today's society. The problem with our education system is that no one has stepped up to the plate to fix it in over a century. The reason it hasn't been fixed is because there's no money behind it. Let me explain.

Our government and big businesses have no interest in providing its citizens a solid education. Political reform is backed by money, and no one is willing to back an education change that won't reap benefits in the private sector for decades. The people within government are simply the puppets who carry out the demands from whoever compensates them.

Most politicians and big businesses want more for themselves and less for the Average Joe. In the past, organizations have wanted compliant employees.

Compliant employees are just smart enough to listen to directions and perform tasks, but just dumb enough to passively accept the shit they receive from their employer. At the end of the day, big organizations and governments don't have a vested interest in making people aware of how poor and irrelevant the American education is. This is why you don't see many lobbyists driving education upgrades.

If there's one thing you can say about millennials, we give the middle finger to "the way things have always been done." Our rebellious nature will hopefully bring reform to our dying education system. If not, it's our kids who will pay the price. We can no longer sit and wait for our government to make changes they should have made decades ago. Why would companies finance a change in our education system? <u>Big businesses only have an interest in financing their own internal education reform</u>. There is no financial benefit for the private sector to fund domestic education across the board. It's much more cost effective for large corporations to effectively train those who directly add to their bottom line. Our education system will continue to suffer because it receives no money from private interests.

Here's something American companies and government haven't wanted in the past: a population of Americans capable of any type of higher cognitive processing. Instead of teaching our youth *how* to think, we tend to teach them *what* to think.

Our education needs to be based around practical concepts that we use in everyday life. Right now, our youth aren't learning about topics that are relevant in today's workplace. We need to be discussing subjects like:

» Teamwork

» Innovation and creative thinking

» Self-development and self-discovery

» Leadership and empowerment

» Compassion

» Philosophy

» Empathy and human emotion

» Leveraging resources and opportunities

» Finances

» Communication (face-to-face)

» Problem solving and critical thinking

» How to design the life you dream of

» Sales and entrepreneurship (because no matter what you do in life, you will be involved in some type of enterprise that buys and sells goods).

These are topics that should be studied in school because they are applicable to our everyday lives. What a concept! This doesn't mean that topics like STEM (Science, Technology, Engineering and Math,) as well as English, should take a back seat. It just means that other subject matters will help these core concepts become more applicable. The reality is, today's students are no longer the people our education system was designed to teach. We have digital immigrant instructors, who speak an outdated language (that of the pre-digital age), [who] are struggling to teach a population that speaks an entirely new language (2). Something needs to change! Today's youth are digital natives – they need to be taught skills that that will be directly applicable to their everyday lives after their formal education ends.

Educating this country has been swept under the rug as an afterthought. Until education reform becomes a *must* item on the to-do list, this country will continue to place under-educated Americans in jobs they're not ready for. Luckily, there are visas like the *H-1B* which allow highly educated immigrants to come and work in the United States (3). There's also a visa for foreign entrepreneurs who want to invest in commercial enterprises called *EB-5* (4). Without these visas, the underfunded education system in America would be forced to show its true colors. These visas have been helping the United States import its innovation since the early 90's.

Fortunately, the digital age has allowed us to privatize (some aspects of) education, and learn practical ideologies from the comfort of our own home (at an affordable price). However, nontraditional methods of education and training are still in their infancy. As market penetration increases for this type of education, many of the traditional methods will be wiped away by lack of demand and large overhead.

Millennials are considered the most educated generation in history. However, high levels of unemployment and student debt have some wondering, "Why did I just get in massive amounts of debt to go searching for a job for a whole year after college?" Many people leave college with zero practical knowledge about what it takes to be successful in the industry of their choice.

However, the culture has again changed. High school graduates today do not have to go to college. Can it be a good idea to go? Absolutely – but it's not for everyone. I know high school graduates who are making six figures a year in industries like real estate and insurance (trades that are considered "intrapreneurial"). Some incredible innovations have come from young adults who are foregoing college for <u>four years of experience over four years of debt</u>.

Our public sector has neglected change in our education system for far too long. It's my belief that education needs massive reform, but I think that initial innovations will come from the private sector, not the government.

The meaning of education has changed over the past twenty years. You can teach yourself nearly anything on YouTube and become proficient over time. Private companies like Udemy, Udacity, Coursera and Khan Academy provide inexpensive and sometimes free courses. You can even take a MOOC (Massive Open Online Course) from one of the Ivy League colleges now– for free. Education has nothing to do with a degree. A degree is just a piece of paper with a seal on it, and apparently, that seal is supposed to give you a sense of credibility. The day I received my college diploma, I realized that the learning process was just beginning.

Education is a lifelong journey, and this generation is looking to their employers for continuous training. Millennials will not be fear mongered into thinking they must stay in a job that's not advancing their career or personal life. Those who are not satisfied with their employers training initiatives will have the choice to take a different path with a more employee focused organization. After all, if there's one thing education has afforded us, it's the right to choose an employer who has our best interests in mind. It'd be nice to see a push from the private sector to institute personal and professional development within an employee's training. But, at the end of the day, every one of us must take personal accountability for our education. We can't expect a broken system to do it for us.

15 ECONOMIC FACTS ABOUT MILLENNIALS. (2014, October). Retrieved November 11, 2016, from

https://www.whitehouse.gov/sites/default/files/docs/
millennials_report.pdf

Published by the Council of Economic Advisors part of the Executive Office of the President of the United States.

Prensky, M. (2001, October 05). Digital Natives, Digital Immigrants. Retrieved December, 2016, from http://www.marc-prensky.com/writing/Prensky%20-%20Digital%20Na-tives,%20Digital%20Immigrants%20-%20Part1.pdf

The H-1B Visa Program: A Primer on the Program and Its Impact on Jobs, Wages, and the Economy. (2016, August 15). Retrieved December, 2016, from https://www.american-immigrationcouncil.org/research/h1b-visa-program-fact-sheet

EB-5 Immigrant Investor Program. (n.d.). Retrieved December, 2016, from https://www.uscis.gov/eb-5

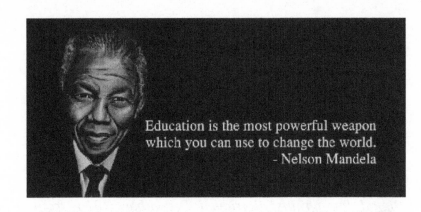

Education is the most powerful weapon which you can use to change the world.
- Nelson Mandela

▪ Politics

A s we venture into controversial territory, we must realize that not everyone feels the same way about these topics – and that's okay. However, I think most people would agree that <u>every election season we end up choosing between *bad and worse* instead of GOOD and GREAT</u>.

The sad reality is that we have a fundamental flaw in our political system. The best leaders in our society are the ones who make great decisions. And, as a society, we hope that politicians will make great decisions on behalf of their constituents – not their bank accounts.

Here's the problem. Trying to work in a broken political system that only serves private interests is a bad decision. But, <u>great leaders make great decisions, which is why they don't become politicians</u>. If we fixed our broken system, then maybe getting involved in politics wouldn't be such a bad idea. Until we see that change, the greatest leaders will typically stay in the private sector because that's where they can have the greatest impact.

For hundreds of years now we have perpetuated a political construct with a huge shortcoming: the party system. John Adams, the first vice president, as well as the second President of the United States, had this to say in a letter to Jonathan Jackson in 1780:

"There is nothing which I dread so much as a division of the republic into two great parties, each arranged under its leader, and concerting measures in opposition to each other. This, in my humble apprehension, is to be dreaded as the greatest political evil under our Constitution" (1).

I know that was an overly complicated quote, but here's the gist of it. <u>A party system will divide this country and create tyranny</u>.

The two-party system we currently have has only perpetuated private interests. Most politicians are prostitutes of the business world. They are bought, sold, and forced to do things based on the money they are given – just like a hooker. You may find that to be an extreme example, but it's the truth.

Are there good politicians out there? Without a doubt. I can think of a few off the top of my head that I'm extremely fond of. However, the great ones can't thrive in a party system that forces them to one side or the other. Most politicians are in the business of going where the money is at. Think of the two major parties as money magnets. Decisions come from the ends of each spectrum because there's no money in the middle. When I hear politicians claim to be in "public service" I laugh. Their business tends to look more like a consulting service.

They have the power to drive public policy, but that policy is typically based on private interests. We tend to consider other countries corrupt, however, in America we have lobbyists, which is more or less a form of legal corruption. Lobbyists sit as the intermediary between the private and public sectors. Their job is to keep everyone's hands clean.

With that said, there are great lobbyists and great politicians who really want to change the world for the better. They stand up for things that need change, and are driven by how that change will positively affect the country. My hat goes off to the good-hearted individuals within the public sector. The problem is that they will never create the change they want under a two-party system because real change goes against both parties' ideologies.

The party system perpetuates gridlock. That's why every conservative ideology is almost the exact opposite of the liberal ideology.

Here's the reality of it: if you're all the way to the left or all the way to the right, you're most likely just looking to pick a fight. Extreme political views to either side means taking a polarizing stance. The reality is, somewhere in the middle is not only bi-partisan; it's pragmatic.

Most of our population is somewhere in the middle. They're just forced to choose a side because of our current party system. Many millennials identify as fiscally conservative and socially liberal. It's thought of as a progressive ideology that stimulates both sides of the table. But is it perfect? Nope.

Here's what's more practical. Two (or three or four) people running as candidates for an election; not candidates of their party, but candidates for president. This would force Americans to educate themselves about all people running, and their stance on different topics. What a concept.

With the party system, people tend to just vote along party lines; in the house, the senate, and in their home. If your parents swing right, you most likely do as well. Voting along party lines just promotes a culture of ignorance. Many people support political candidates to keep the opposition out of office. The "lesser of two evils" election will continue to happen until we decide to make a change to our political system. <u>We must go from voting for parties to voting for leaders</u>. It's my hope that the millennials lead this change.

Business Insider created a video to put the entire U.S. population into perspective using the average of 100 people (2). Twenty-nine of them identified as democrat, 26 of them identified as republican, 42 of them identified as independent and 3 did not have an opinion. Unfortunately, out of those same 100 people, only 58 of them voted for president (based on the 2012 election). The people who tend to not vote are the same ones who feel that their voices won't be heard – the 42 people who are independent thinkers. The 55% of the population who identify with a particular party typically vote to keep the other party out, not their party in. If all the independent thinkers banded together, the two-party system would end, and a new political era would begin.

So, here's what happens in an average presidential election. About half the country votes and someone from one of the big parties gets elected. Half the country (or more) complains about how terrible this president is because they're not moving the country forward, just progressing their political agendas. Half of Americans vote and half of those votes go to the winning party. This means that only (about) 25% of the country votes for our president. The president's vision only extends as far as the followers who feel the same way, which is a small minority of the country.

The checks and balances system both works for us and against us. It protects us from tyranny but also limits our progress. The democrats need the republicans and the republicans need the democrats. It's a co-dependent relationship. Without the other party, what is there to argue about?

All the party system does is divide this country. John Adams said it in the 1700's, and it's just as true today.

It's my belief that the party system will fall in good time. It's corrupt, and many changes to the American

<u>(and global) economy won't happen until we have a leader that has the best interest of the people – not their party, their pockets, or their ability to get reelected</u>.

Unfortunately, politics has a long lifespan. After people finish their careers in the private sector, they think it's a good idea to hold public office until they roll over in their grave. Typically, politics ends up being a bunch of retired millionaires (or billionaires) who are making decisions on behalf of working class people one or two generations below them. Don't like it? Sorry, that's how it works.

Fixing a broken system requires change, and change starts with great leadership. The problem is that great leadership won't enter the political arena until the change happens. It's a catch-22. Leaders go where they have the greatest opportunity to create change, and until the party system collapses, great leaders will remain in the private sector.

We need an ideological movement in this country. A movement that promotes a foundation of:

» Leveraged resources for American people and companies to thrive upon.

» An individualistic way of thinking (which requires us to move away from organized religion and politics). A government that promotes its citizens to create their own belief systems.

» Building of communities and ecosystems that give people a place to connect.

» Human rights, and the ability to make personal choices.

» Equality, not sameness.

» Tax rates and credits that incentivize corporations and individuals to increase spending and investing in American commerce.

» Complete self-awareness and individual enlightenment.

» A modernized education system that teaches practical skills that will provide a foundation for our youth.

» Public programs that provide well balanced medical and social resources.

» International relations that promotes free trade and global cooperation.

» Investments in renewable infrastructure like solar, hemp, water desalination, and hybrid transportation.

» Supercharging marginalized communities with resources that provide a tangible foundation for Americans.

» And deregulation of some, but not all, industries to promote economic growth. The government doesn't create economies; individuals and companies do.

Most of these things are not in the best interest of any politician. Imagine if there were a political platform based on things like resourcefulness, human rights, technological advancement, inclusion, abundance, and free thought. Politicians would no longer be forced to think about what side of the table they sit on; they'd be forced to think about what will benefit the American people. This type of philosophy doesn't lock into the conservative or liberal ideologies; it locks into the premise of the 21st century: resourcefulness, tractability, individual enlightenment, and economic expansion. The old system has existed for far too long. It's time for a new age ideology that puts citizens first.

Millennials are looking to make a logical shift in our political culture. Maybe this political shift will happen in 20 years – that would be nice. Maybe it'll happen in ten. Maybe in five. Maybe tomorrow. Who knows? All I know is that political change is a must, and something that will happen in the future. You can count on it.

John Adams, Letter to Jonathan Jackson, October 1780. (2012, December 01). Retrieved January, 2017, from http://thefederalistpapers.org/founders/adams/john-adams-letter-to-jonathan-jackson-october-1780

Kuzoian, A. (2016, May 12). This animation puts the entire US population into perspective. Retrieved December, 2016, from http://www.businessinsider.com/the-united-states-as-100-people-2016-5

◼ Religion

Just as controversial as politics, there is a religious revolution happening not only in America, but around the world.

There have been many articles written about how millennials are ruining Christianity (1). They're not ruining it. Millennials just aren't as religious as their elders. To many millennials, the word "god" has to do with spirituality, not religion. We tend to be independent thinkers who have created our own ideologies about what "god" means to us. It's my opinion that our society is less religious than it has ever been, yet at the same time, more spiritual than it has ever been. I expect both trends to continue over time.

Organized religion is on its way out the door, and rightfully so. Organized religion is predicated on texts written thousands of years ago. Religious texts are someone's opinions that some people now consider facts. With that said, there's no doubt in my mind that these texts will retain their historical value for centuries to come.

I was fortunate enough to study successful people from a very early age. I learned something life altering while working as a speaker for Tony Robbins. The most successful people on the planet are the ones who can change the beliefs that no longer serve them any time they choose. I didn't get it until an old belief bit me in the butt.

I used to have beliefs years ago that I now consider crazy. Beliefs about business, or friends, or money, or politics. When I realized that those beliefs didn't hold true for me any longer, I changed the belief to my new psychological construct – what I thought to be a new empowering belief.

While at one of Tony Robbins's events, I realized that my beliefs will continue to change, grow and evolve based on my life's experiences, and the experiences of others. This was a profound epiphany at the time. But today, I know this to be true.

I look at scriptures from thousands of years ago – the Bible, the Torah, the Koran – and I respect these texts. They are works of art and a part of our history. However, can you honestly say that you believe every word in whichever text is applicable to you? To believe in an old belief system that was only applicable at the time it was written seems problematic.

Why would I tie myself to a belief system that someone else wrote for me? Is that egotistical? Absolutely not. That's smart. I choose my beliefs. I choose which ones stay, which ones go, and which ones get edited. <u>Having that choice gives me personal power and total control</u> (TC – something we'll discuss later).

Organized religion is just that – organized. It's another way to separate you from me, and show others how they are wrong and you are right.

The truth is that no one is right or wrong because we can't prove anything. That's part of the inherent beauty of spirituality and religion. It's part of an individual's philosophy.

I had someone ask me if I was Jewish or Catholic, and I looked at them like they were crazy. I said, "I'm not Jewish, Catholic, Muslim, Democrat or Republican – I'm Jesse Henry." The look on their face went blank. It was like they had never conceptualized creating their own philosophy. They had always followed the path someone else set forth for them. Most people who practice organized religion never change because they believe what was told to them from a young age. Over people's lives, religion has changed from something they do to becoming part of who they are. However, what was taught to you is not always good for you. Creating a belief system that will help you grow today and tomorrow will always be a formula for success.

I'm not talking down to anyone that is religious. I have many friends who have vowed themselves to a faith. Whatever works for you, works for you. What works for me, works for me. I have personal beliefs that can be found in religious scriptures, and there is a chance that those beliefs are so foundational that they will never evolve.

I also believe that many millennials have changed the word "god" (in their personal vocabulary) to "higher power" or "higher energy." Do I believe in a higher energy? Yes, energy is infinite. It is beyond and within. It is everywhere and nowhere (2). All the energy in our universe can't be explained, quantified, or seen. It can also not be created nor destroyed. But, the belief in a higher power has absolutely nothing to do with religion. That's why people mistake their philosophies for religions and religions as facts. Many people believe in a higher energy – call it God, call it aliens, or call it Einstein. It doesn't matter. Millennials tend to believe that we shouldn't stick to religious constructs because "that's how it's always been." Everyone has a spiritual side, but not everyone has a religious side.

Organized politics and religion are both ways to separate society. It makes you different from me. It makes my way right and your way wrong. That's a zero-sum game, and one that's never going to allow you to live life on your own terms.

We should not let others write our rules and beliefs for us, we should be the creators of our own philosophical perspective. Creating your own definition for religion, God, spirituality, politics, or anything else for that matter, is an empowering activity. Millennials will never be truly happy adopting social constructs that "have always been." Independent thinking is the new path to enlightenment. What's always been may not be as applicable in today's world. Creating your own belief system allows you to embrace the principles that you find empowering *today*. As humans, we should be constantly going through a philosophical iteration process where we challenge our beliefs to see if they can (or should) be replaced.

Challenging the norm isn't just fun, it's constructive. Therefore, organized politics and religion are on their way out, and a new individualistic way of thinking is on its way in.

Are Millennials Destroying Christianity? (2015, May 13). Retrieved December, 2016, from https://www.youtube.com/watch?v=nMCH8GzILIM

Max Loughan 13 year old physicist, Inventor has New Theory on God. (2016, August 19). Retrieved January 07, 2017, from https://www.youtube.com/watch?v=wn5bKALeSyM

■ Money

Money. Money. Money. It smells nice. It feels nice. It helps us buy nice things. But, did you really wake up as a kid dreaming of acquiring a bunch of pieces of paper with dead people on it? I hope not – that's a pretty morbid goal. Most of the generations before us did exactly that. They worked half their lives to make money, and hoped that their efforts would buy them happiness.

Or how about commas in your bank account? As a kid, did you think that you would judge people based on their online banking balance? Probably not.

Then, something happened. We grew up, started sensationalizing "successful" personalities and spent our lives trying to figure out how to keep up with the Joneses.

Millennials have nothing against the Joneses. I'm sure they're really nice people. However, don't assume that the Joneses are *both happy and successful* just because they live in a nice house. The truth is, just because people have lots of money doesn't necessarily mean they have a quality life. Money is a tool and tools give us leverage. If we think money is the ultimate source of our happiness, then we'll never be truly satisfied. We may search for money for the rest of our lives and never discover the happiness that was right in front of our faces.

Let's use an example:

Professional A: Makes $1.75 million per year, drives a nice car, divorced, has a large business with a high burn rate and frequently stresses that he's "not enough."

Professional B: Makes $65,000 per year, loving family, one vacation each summer, stable job, plays sports on the weekends and always has friends coming over.

Who is more successful? Well, by traditional standards, Professional A. I mean, he's rich! He can buy whatever he wants, whenever he wants. Who cares if he's divorced? There are plenty of fish in the sea.

Here's the problem. We're led to believe that money makes us happy. The thought process was always "get rich, so we can buy what we want."

What happens is, we go and swipe our credit card for this shiny object. We play with it for a couple of weeks. Then, suddenly, it's not so shiny anymore. What do we do? We go swipe our card to by another "shinier object." Money allows us to sustain a lifestyle and a sense of freedom, but too often people define themselves based on the balance in their bank account.

During my speaking engagements, I can tell you with 100% confidence and certainty that I've met just as many depressed rich people as depressed poor people. The problem is, if we're depressed when we're poor, we're going to be depressed when we're rich. Money isn't going to solve our depression. Neither will anti-depressants. If we want to be happy, we must fix our mindset and realize that happiness is a choice (and so is success).

Money can be a complete trap. People become enslaved to their money because it's a game they can't win. The number just gets bigger and bigger, and we just end up wanting more and more.

Love it or hate it, money is the root of most of our problems, but it can also be the solution if properly allocated. Money just helps us become more of who we already are. If we're an asshole, we just become a bigger asshole. If we're a leader, we become more of a leader.

However, we must realize that <u>the reason we want money is for the specific emotion it will illicit within us</u>. Most people want money because they think it will give them power, confidence, certainty, inspiration, freedom, or any other positive emotion.

Here's the reality of it: we can attain all those emotions by doing something else. We were just led to believe that money is the quickest way to achieve the emotional states we desire. The reality is, all the emotions we desire are free.

I'm not saying that money is a bad thing. I believe in the free market, and that capitalism has created the world's most powerful movements. Everyone has the right to the pursuit of profit. Money can change our lives. Hell, it can change the world!

But, money is easy to come and easy to go. It can help us grow and flourish. It can help us create magical moments. It can help us employ people, and it can help us change others' lives.

Know this, though: money will not fix all our problems (unless you're in serious financial debt). However, once the debt is paid off, the next problem will arise. If you're looking to avoid problems by becoming rich, realize that problems when you're wealthy are both large and expensive.

Overall, our generation doesn't value money as highly today as previous generations did at this age. As the millennial generation ages, money will naturally become more of a priority. We'll start to get married, which means buying houses and having kids. Millennials realize that even when money becomes a necessity, it does not define us as individuals.

Money will not solve a problem for us. If we have problems in our lives, then we need to look from within for the power and means to change. I know people with tons of money who are *mentally and emotionally homeless.* True riches can't be bought, because being rich is a choice. Being successful is a choice. We can be rich in our relationships, rich in our health and rich in our decisions. Rich isn't something we become, it's something we are. There's nothing worse than seeing a wealthy person who is depressed. If we're mentally rich, money will be the least of our concerns. Thinking that $1 million will make you successful is a trap. Decide to be successful today, instead of having it be something you attain "one day." The attainment of money is just another form of "destination addiction." This is the belief that happiness is tied to a future outcome, which prevents people living in a state of pleasure in this current moment. If you're really looking to make more money, then the solution is simple. People make money by making decisions. The more important the decisions are, the more money you'll acquire. If you want to make more money, start by making more important decisions. The power of decision is what gives us the power to attain anything we want in this world.

Many millennials want to become wealthy, myself included, but to get that $1 million (or whatever that number is for us) we must do something, or perform some type of action. However, to do what needs to be done, we must become the type of person that can actually do it. In other words: in order to *get* you must *do,* but in order to do you must *become.*

We need to stop looking for the $1 million and start focusing on becoming the type of person who can become a millionaire. The person we become by making that money will last a lot longer than the $1 million. Instead of focusing on the money, we must focus on developing our identity, or our personal philosophy and uniqueness. The type of person who makes a million dollars has a very strong set of beliefs and patterns that help them conquer any feat. If we want to emulate another person's success, we must start by looking deep within that individual's philosophy for proper insight.

Always remember that to *become* the person we see down the road, we must *be. Being present* is something that's been lost in translation in today's world. When we are just *being*, we're self-aware and mindful of everything around us. Technology has taken us out of the present moment of our own lives, and put us in the presence of others around the world.

However, having the self-awareness to push ourselves mentally and physically every day is what will make us successful. That's what will make us wealthy. And, that's what will allow us to go to sleep a happy camper. Everyone looks at money a little differently, especially individuals in the millennial generation. To keep money in perspective, we need to remember that the destination is the journey, and true wealth is just a byproduct of doing good for others along the way.

P.S. – If you're wealthy, ask yourself: "Am I rich? Or do I just have a lot of money?"

■ Values

Quite frankly, millennials don't do what we're supposed to do, or what we should do – we do what we want to do (and we're ridiculed for it). We do what we want because it helps us attain the values we desire. Unfortunately, personal and professional values are frequently overlooked within an organization. If corporate values align with our personal values, what you need done is what we will want to get done!

Any successful relationship, whether it's a business relationship, friendship, or marriage, is based off communication. The most successful relationships are the ones where both parties properly align and communicate their values to each other.

I had never sat down and thought about my values until I hit a brick wall during my first job out of college. Unfortunately, I learned this lesson the hard way.

I've always been an entrepreneur. When I was a kid, it was selling candy or scrap metal. When I was in college it was koozies, video production and even insurance for a while. When it came time to graduate, though, I didn't know what to do. All I knew was that I wanted to be successful. Success was my highest value. I thought, "Hey, if I'm successful, then everything else will fall into place."

However, everyone told me the same story over and over – go work under someone else to "learn the biz." I must have heard it 100 times before having a conversation with Bob Davis, founder of Lycos and successful venture capitalist. He brought his company from inception to IPO in nine months at the peak of the dot com bubble. I figured he would have some quality advice for me.

While speaking with Bob, he mentioned something that caught my attention. He, along with everyone else, also suggested that I work under someone, even if it was for a short period of time. However, he mentioned one piece specifically that got me hooked. He revealed the concept of skipping the line. He said that if I worked under someone for a few years, I could learn the ropes much quicker and get a large company perspective before going off on my own. Made sense, right?

So, I listened to him. After I gave my TEDx Talk (two months before graduation), I decided to learn the ropes from one employer and one employer only. Tony Robbins. Millennials may know him as "banana hands" from *Shallow Hal,* but boomers and Generation X know him as the guy from the infomercials or "one of the greatest motivational speakers of all time." Everyone told me I was too young to be a speaker. But, when someone in business tells me "no," the only answer I'm telling myself is, "just wait and see."

So, I became one of Tony Robbins eight "peak performance strategists." I was a national speaker who got to travel around the country giving corporate trainings to small organizations, as well as Fortune 500 companies. I was on track to make mid-six figures a year as a 23-year-old straight out of college. I had "skipped the line" by all means of the definition. Sounds pretty bad-ass, right? It was – until it wasn't. I absolutely despised the situation I was in. I was running a script for my workshop that I felt was not allowing me to perform as the best version of myself. I wanted to be the show when I was speaking, but my job wasn't to be the show. My job was to spend an hour gradually leading someone down the path of purchasing the show – a three-and-a half-day event with Tony Robbins. I loved the man I worked for, and the message I shared, but I knew I had more of my own potential to tap into.

I felt like a phony. I was a peak performance strategist that wasn't at my own peak performance. I was tired, sad, frustrated, annoyed, and angry at the situation. I was heading down a road to depression and felt completely helpless.

While I was sorting through l my papers one day, I freaked out and threw them on the counter in frustration. I put my face in my hands and said, "All I want is to be happy – why is that so hard?!"

And, all of a sudden, it clicked. I was chasing the wrong value. I wanted to be successful so badly that once I was considered successful (by other people's standards), I wasn't happy. In that very moment, my number one value changed from success to happiness. I realized that I didn't want success at the cost of my happiness. So, the big question in my life changed from "How do I become successful?" to "How do I become happy?" There was only one logical answer to that question: quit my job!

I picked up the phone, called my boss and put in my two weeks. It was that easy. I didn't think of repercussions. I didn't think of how I was going to get my next paycheck. I just thought about being happy. I woke up the next morning and I felt 50 pounds lighter. It was like I had found the path to enlightenment. Whenever I'm feeling down, I think about the morning after I quit my job. I was on cloud nine. It's a feeling that will stick with me for the rest of my life.

I ended up starting my own company and found my way, just like I had in all my other ventures. However, upon reflection, I haven't been an entrepreneur my whole life because I wanted to be successful. I have been an entrepreneur because it's what makes me happy. And to me, happiness is the key to life. You can have all the money in the world, but if you're not happy, then what's the point?

I learned this lesson the hard way. My friends ridiculed me for throwing away an opportunity that any other college graduate (and most working professionals) would have died for. I hit a slump after quitting and missed out on my first couple of deals because of my own mistakes. It took longer than I expected to get the ball rolling. But, when the going got tough, I brought myself back to that feeling of pure ecstasy the morning after I had quit. I realized that my values are what I hold closest to my heart. Strong values will drive people to do things they don't realize they are capable of doing.

I'm beyond grateful that I took the advice Bob Davis gave me during the summer of 2014. Working under Tony Robbins not only shortened my learning curve, but brought me to a place of self-actualization. Tony taught me things that can't be learned in a classroom. I could better understand who I was, what I wanted, why I felt the way I felt, and how I was going to get everything I ever wanted. None of those realizations would have come to fruition if I didn't experience the pain and frustration working under someone else. In my case, these were lessons that were meant to be learned the hard way.

If you're the owner or manager of an organization, you must understand and internalize exactly which values your company stands for. After you discover those values, you need to look for those values in your employees and potential new hires. You may face a loyalty challenge if you don't find employees with similar values to yours.

Can you get along with someone who has different values? Absolutely, but you need to have authenticity and honesty, and realize that not every good person is a good employee.

Your values also extend to your customers. Find clients that share your values and you'll have a lot easier time marketing and selling to them. In today's world, your customers are your employees, and your employees are your customers.

Employees should be using your product, and your customers should be evangelizing your product. If they aren't, it's possible that there is a misalignment in values.

A good way to catalyze this transparency is to display your company values (or personal ones) in a way that everyone can see. Maybe it's on your website, your desk, your wall, or your email signature. It's extremely beneficial to have the constant reminder that *this* is what you're driving toward. It'll help you find and connect more people with those same interests. Companies are starting to wake up to the realization that articulating their corporate mission and values is not fluff (1). Steve Jobs did a great job reiterating the values and vision when the going got tough. He made sure that both employees and customers understood exactly what Apple stood for. This is how Apple became a powerhouse under his leadership.

Before we move on, I must warn you that at a moment's notice your values can change. It doesn't matter whether it's a value you want to move towards or a value that you want to move away from. It's important to realize that as humans we change, grow, and adapt. We're a product of our nature and nurturing, and sometimes our nurturing leads us to a place of change. This isn't a bad thing – it's just a reality of life.

Mainwaring, S. (n.d.). What Steve Jobs Knew About the Importance of Values to Your Company We First Branding. Retrieved January, 2016, from http://wefirstbranding.com/brands/what-steve-jobs-knew-about-the-importance-of-values-to-your-company/

Activity

Write down the top three values you want to move towards, and the top three values you want to move away from.

Typical Toward Values: Love, Success, Freedom, Intimacy, Security, Adventure, Power, Passion, Comfort, Health, Ambition, Balance, Safety, Confidence, Creativity, Integrity, Humor, Honesty, Approval, Happiness, Growth, Fun, Freedom, Flexibility, Excitement, Respect, Learning, Optimism, Trust, Achievement.

Typical Away Values: Rejection, Anger, Blame, Frustration, Loneliness, Depression, Failure, Humiliation, Guilt, Disappointment, Shame, Panic, Helplessness, Bigotry, Cheating, Indecisiveness, Deception, Inferiority, Stress, Conflict, Jealousy, Dishonesty, Embarrassment, Neediness, Egotistical, Weakness, Resentfulness, Complaining, Disrespect.

My Top Three Toward Values:

1. _____

2. _____

3. _____

My Top Three Away Values:

1. _____

2. _____

3. _____

Understanding your values will help you understand why you make decisions time and time again.

Understanding the values of others will also help you understand why they make the decisions they make.

If you're working with (or selling to) a millennial, start by understanding their values and how you can help them attain the emotional states they truly desire.

■ Entrepreneurship

I t is with great pride and pleasure that I can make this statement: Millennials are the most entrepreneurial generation of all time (1). It gave me chills just writing it.

The U.S. Chamber of Commerce has this to say about millennials:

"Millennials score high on IQ tests. They also score higher on such traits as extraversion, self-esteem, self-liking, high expectations and assertiveness. These traits are purported to often lead to narcissism and entitlement."

The narcissistic and entitled millennials are more inclined to have excessive social media usage. But, you and I both know that there are narcissistic and entitled people in *every* generation. Quite often, these negative traits are carried out because of someone's need to feel like an individual. Overall, these traits tend to be prominent in the most successful entrepreneurs. That innate desire to create something unique and beneficial for society is why this generation will make entrepreneurial advances we never thought possible. Millennials approach entrepreneurship not as a career, but as a way of life. Previous generations dreamed of climbing up the corporate ladder. Millennials dream of creating something extraordinary. Over time, this generation will become the most seasoned entrepreneurial leaders the world has seen thus far.

Starting a business today has never been so easy. It's less expensive, less risky, and there is an abundance of opportunities to become wealthy. There has been a huge movement in minority communities to step up to the entrepreneurial plate, and the blurring of gender roles have opened the doors to so much more potential. Any person who wants to be an entrepreneur can do so. It's a choice. Lowering the barriers to entry is the best thing that could have happened to entrepreneurship.

The Internet has singlehandedly leveled the playing field. Thomas Friedman, journalist, author, and three time Pulitzer Prize winner, spoke about this extensively in his book about globalization, *The World is Flat*. He speaks of 10 flatteners which have shaped 21st century economies: the fall of the Berlin Wall, the rise of Netscape, workflow software, uploading, outsourcing, offshoring, supply-chaining, insourcing, informing, and finally "The Steroids" (2). The section on "Informing" references resources like Google and Wikipedia, which have helped spread information across the world. "The Steroids" refers to wireless technology like mobile phones. He references the digital, mobile, personal, and virtual movement as something that has permanently altered our society. Modern day entrepreneurs are building off the foundation of the ten flatteners, which have allowed start-ups to compete with major players in each industry.

Although big business still takes a majority of a given market's profits, there's still enough meat on the bone in nearly every industry to make money. Create a new offering or innovate an old one, find a customer, and you're in business.

When new technological advances are made, who tends to be the early adopters of the product? Millennials. We want to try it, test it, critique it and enhance it. We feel that it's our duty to make technology useful and beneficial to those who use it.

We're entering an age where *anyone* can start a business. Seventy-two percent of millennials aspire to be their own boss one day (3). Will many of these people fail? How many of these entrepreneurs will persevere through that failure? Only time will tell.

I caution blind optimism for those who think entrepreneurship is a fairy tale. Too many people look at entrepreneurship as some glamorous, easy living lifestyle, but it's far from the truth – to a certain extent.

Can you start a business, become successful and only put in a few hours a week? It may take a lot of time and energy to get it to that point, but, yes, you can. If that's what you're looking to do, I recommend checking out Tim Ferriss' book, *4 Hour Work Week.* It's a classic.

Books like Tim's have caused a rise in "lifestyle entrepreneurship," which is work-life balance manifested into a profit. The fundamental principle here is separating "how you make money" from "how you spend your time." These are entrepreneurs who only need a laptop and internet connection to manage their business (4). Sounds pretty cool, right?

Well, it is, and there are many people making six figures and traveling the world while their business self-sustains. If you're looking to build a true empire, then this probably isn't the best route. For some people, though, this is "livin' the dream."

Two of the millennial entrepreneurs who lead the pack are Evan Spiegel (Snapchat) and Mark Zuckerberg (Facebook). These gentlemen showed our generation that you can take an idea, turn it into a business, and make billions. They're the unicorns, along with Uber, Airbnb, and a few others. The people that found these companies used the millennial ideology to create something spectacular.	Interconnectedness.	Collaboration. Relationships. Globalization. And most of all, creating a unique experience for their users. This is what 21st century entrepreneurship is all about.

If you want to build one of these empires, you and I are on the same page. Right here. Right now. And, if you want to build an empire, this is the only piece of advice you will ever need.

> *"You MUST be willing to take the next step forward right now."*
>
> JH

If you want to become successful, you must always look for improvement, both personally and professionally. Taking the next step is what separates the entrepreneurs from the wantrapreneurs. Success is just an iteration of many failures.

Some executives may be saying, "How does this apply to me? Are you saying that all my employees will eventually quit and become my competitors?" Not necessarily.

Many business owners and managers have created an "intrapreneurial" culture within their organization. Doing this gives employees a sense of autonomy and possession over their work. Millennials want to feel like they're creating something of their own, and your business can help support them in doing so.

Entrepreneurship is about more than owning a business. It's about building something incredible. It's about adding value to others. And, it's about having total and complete control over your destiny.

Asghar, R. (2014, November 11). Study: Millennials Are The True Entrepreneur Generation. Retrieved December, 2016, from http://www.forbes.com/sites/robasghar/2014/11/11/ study-millennials-are-the-true-entrepreneur-generation/#3d9cbf4e5e92

Tom Friedman's Ten Flatteners and Triple Convergence. (2008, August 05). Retrieved December, 2016, from http://hatman2.blogspot.com/2008/08/tom-friedmans-ten-flatteners.html

Gallup. (2005, April 12). Majority of Americans Want to Start Own Business. Retrieved December, 2016, from http://www.gallup.com/poll/15832/majority-americans-want-start-own-business.aspx

Constable, K. (2015, April 06). 6 Steps to Becoming a Lifestyle Entrepreneur. Retrieved December, 2016, from https://www.entrepreneur.com/article/244407

■ Total Control – (TC)

We have a large problem in this country, and that is total control itself. It's both the problem and solution in our lives. Millennials are looking for more ways to take total control over their own destiny. We want control over our work, our health, our beliefs, our relationships and anything else that can have a significant impact on our lives. Company executives need to look to create a scope of work for employees that gives total control to the individuals pursuit of growth, while maintaining total control over their organization's destiny.

Total control has a happy medium. It's useful in some situations, and destructive in others. As humans, we tend to give total control to those more capable than ourselves. We give it to our government, and they accept it with open arms. They need to have total control because without it, what do they really have? The easiest way for both governments and corporations to gain total control is to use fear. They want us to think that we need them, which gives them total control.

Governmental control has led the United States to become the most incarcerated nation in the world (1). That's a fact (at least today). Many people in jails aren't villains. They're just mentally ill Americans that our government disguises as criminals.

The general population has given total control to not only the government, but also the companies who bridge the gap between the public and private sector. The healthcare industry doesn't make money when we are healthy. They only make money when we are sick. Take a moment and think about that conflict of interest. Our health is in the hands of someone who wants to make money off us. To make money off us, they need us to stay (or become) sick. The healthcare industry has total control over some of the public health issues we face in everyday society.

No singular problem is the cause of all our suffering. These issues are all multi-dimensional. However, all of these problems are a result of our government and corporations wanting total and complete control. They want us to think they're keeping us safe, but they're just herding sheep.

Many people have the misconception that millennials are antigovernment, or anarchists. This is not true; we just have a strong belief that our government should have total control over some things, and limited control over others.

Total control is a concept that most people fear, and rightfully so. If we have total control, then we're responsible for both our successes and our failures. That's a good thing. Many people want us to think that if we take total control, we're destined for failure. This is a tactic that's used in marketing and other forms of pain (or fear) driven propaganda.

Religion, politics, and healthcare are in the business of taking control. As a population, we allow them to take control because it gives us the opportunity to dish the blame on something else. "Oh, this is just what God had planned" or "It's okay, it was out of our control."

I challenge you to take total and complete control over your destiny. Will there be situations that are left up to chance? Yup. There are just some things in life that we won't have control over. We must accept the things in life that are out of our control, but also realize that we tend to give up control because it's convenient to put our fate in someone else's hands. For people who are used to being in total control, accepting that sometimes "shit happens" can be the hardest obstacle to overcome. In this case, acceptance means coming to terms that we may not have control over everything that happens in our lives. When this happens, we have the opportunity to control our focus, the meaning we give things, and most importantly, what we're going to do about it. We can't control circumstances, but we can always control our reactions.

The easiest way to take total control over our lives is to become self-aware, and self-awareness sits on a mental, physical, emotional, and spiritual foundation. There are many within this generation who are not self-aware of who they are, what they want, and what they're doing about it. They just go about life living vicariously through social media figures and fanaticizing about what life could be if they actually put in the work. There are other millennials who internalize these influencers philosophies to drive them forward; therefore, taking total control.

However, sometimes our need for total control can nip us in the butt. When in a relationship or business partnership, you want to shy away from becoming a "control freak." There is something to be said for people who like to be in the driver's seat, but who can also trust their partners to take the wheel when need be. Total control is only good if you're conscientious of when to let go. Too much control will make you a control freak. Too little control will make you a puppet. Mindfulness will tell you when it's appropriate to be a player or a spectator.

Being self-aware will help you determine the right time to take control and the right time to give it.

Total control starts with taking 100% accountability for our actions. Don't hope or pray for something to happen. Go make it happen! No one will get you that promotion, that incredible partnership you've always yearned for, or that trip around the world. That's all on you!

Wishing and praying will never get us results. The people sitting there waiting for that "amazing opportunity" do *not* have total control. The people willing to act and go create that opportunity *are* taking total control. Those are the ones who want destiny in their hands and not in someone else's.

There are so many sheep in this world and it's easy to get herded into generalizations that make us feel like we're losing control. Just remember that no one can take our control away from us; we have to give it to them. That's right – we literally have to hand over control to someone else. That, my friends, is a choice. It seems that millennials are more aware of total control and how it's used for both the good and the bad.

If we've been in a situation where we felt helpless or felt like we didn't have a choice, it's because we didn't make decisions at the forefront that allowed us to retain control over our own destiny. When we lose control, it's not time to blame others; it's time to look in the mirror to see how we can improve the next time around.

Highest to Lowest Prison Population Total. (n.d.). Retrieved December, 2016, from http://www.prisonstudies.org/highest-to-lowest/prison-population-total?field_region_taxonomy_tid=All

What We Have

Understanding and Appreciating Versus Judging and Advising

Are there some millennials that are schmucks? Of course there are. There are schmucks in every generation, race, religion and political party. Multi-generational workforces need to work together to be understood as individuals; not herded into generalizations that perpetuate disengagement.

One of the worst things an elder can do is judge or advise someone in this generation on how to live their life. This tends to tell us that you think we're inadequate to make our own decisions to further our own lives. Unless it's asked for, judging and advising just creates animosity. It's a red flag for disaster.

Coming from a place of understanding and appreciating is the empathetic 21st century solution to every problem. Asking questions, and discovering why something is the way it is, will give you the insight you need to make the right decisions. This holds true for both millennials and the generations that surround them.

The better the questions we ask ourselves, the better the answers we'll get. So, before we decide to jump the gun and tell someone how they should act, let's find out why they're acting that way.

We may learn something we didn't know previously. Sometimes, it's better to ask people the appropriate question so our counterpart has the opportunity to uncover their own solution. Telling someone what to do could put them in that fight or flight mode.

Am I saying that that we can never advise someone? No. I'm saying that it's important to understand before we advise. Once we advise, we should go back to understanding to see how they responded to the advice. It's an ebb and a flow, a cyclical movement between trial, error, self-awareness and retrial. We all need to become conscientious about how our actions are going to affect the actions of our counterparts. When we're controlling our actions, we're in control of our destiny. Most of life's problems arise because we're either acting without thinking, or thinking without acting. If we're always listening and thinking before we act, all our actions will be efficient and purposeful. This is how we can effectively use total control to grow and flourish over time.

Active listening is one of those important skills that's not taught in schools. We must make sure we're <u>listening to understand, not to respond</u>. Clearly understanding before responding is something most people don't take the time to do. If we're always looking to understand, we will avoid judgment and realize that everyone has their reasons for doing what they do. It's important to look for those reasons before we advise others on the actions they should take. We should always remember that there are "different strokes for different folks" – everyone is unique. Good advice for one person may be bad advice for another.

The best way to summarize this ideology is to quote Mary Schmich of the Chicago Tribune. She wrote an essay that's supposed to be read as a graduation speech. The final three sentences are as follows:

"Be careful whose advice you buy, but be patient with those who supply it. Advice is a form of nostalgia. Dispensing it is a way of fishing the past from the disposal, wiping it off, painting over the ugly parts and recycling it for more than it's worth" **(1).**

Schmich, M. (2009, May 13). Advice, like youth, probably just

wasted on the young. Retrieved December, 2016, from http://www.chicagotribune.com/news/columnists/chischmich-sunscreen-column-column.html

■ Motivation

Millennials are easy to motivate and easy to discourage. Understanding a millennial's values can help us influence them into unprecedented action. However, a lack of understanding will cause miscommunication, and ultimately distrust. The great news is that millennials want to be motivated, which makes the process smooth if executed properly.

People are motivated by either moving away from pain or toward pleasure. This is premised on the basic principles of conditioning, where people seek more of what's rewarded, and less of what is punished (1). Marketers today must walk a fine line between motivating their customers with pain, and making them feel like shit. The same holds true for employees, and anyone else for that matter. Some people associate pain to going to the gym, while others associate pleasure. Understanding how individuals perceive and associate pain and pleasure will help us move anyone toward (or away from) any action. These principles are based on human psychology and biology.

I once had a boss that told me that there was only one way to do it, and if I didn't do it that way, then I wouldn't have a job. It was his way or the highway. How's that for motivation?

Besides the fact that he was blatantly wrong (there was more than one way to accomplish the same goal, as there are with most things in life), he was commanding instead of asking. If he had asked me about some other strategies I felt were effective, we could have had a discussion and landed at the right answer. Even if his solution ended up being correct, I still would have been satisfied. However, the fact that he thought he knew his answer was the only answer, and wasn't open to discussing other possibilities, showed me how *not* to manage and motivate my future subordinates.

Millennials need some sense of autonomy. Yes, we understand that there are processes in place to help us succeed. But, we can't automatically assume that our way is the right way, just because it's our way. That's not how successful companies are run. Asking, understanding, and collaborating on solutions shows thoughtfulness and alignment. If my boss had asked for my opinion, the conversation would have been a lot more empowering. I was looking for reasons why, and the only reason I had heard was "because that's the way it's always been done." Remember, in the 21st century, those words are the kiss of death.

Motivation is about empowering your team to make decisions and ask questions. Sometimes we could stumble upon a new, innovative solution that could help the rest of the team succeed. No company will ever discover new systems if their answer is "because that's the way it's always been done." If we're the leader that's always talking, we'll eventually be surrounded by employees who are never talking. It's time to start asking questions, and tap into the potential of those around us.

Our generation loves asking the question "why," and it seems to piss people off. However, most people are motivated and fulfilled when they know the reasoning behind something. Millennials want to understand the process, and how that process can be improved or changed to create better results. If we don't challenge the traditions of our past, we will never create a better future.

This whole book is about how to motivate and communicate with millennials. Millennials are typically motivated by experiences that are emotionally satisfying. However, motivation isn't just something a company does. It's something that must be ingrained in their culture. It must be core to our company's ideologies, and it must be centered around open and transparent communication. Regardless if you're a millennial or not, motivation can significantly change the trajectory of your life. Others can pump you up and motivate you all they want, but never forget that real change and real motivation comes from within.

Pleasure-Pain Principle. (n.d.). Retrieved December, 2016, from http://changingminds.org/disciplines/psychoanalysis/concepts/pleasure_pain.htm

■ Ambition

Millennials tend to be ambitious, but ambition is a double-edged sword. Earlier I explained how my values changed from success to happiness. I was so amped up to become successful, that I completely forgot about everything else in my life.

I've always said that the most important trait that I'm looking for in a significant other is ambition. Yes, I would like my wife to have a great personality and be charismatic, funny and beautiful – but who wouldn't? All those things come secondary.

Ambition is sexy and it's what I look for not only in a significant other, but any type of partnership. Whether they're friends, business partners, co-workers or associates, I'm looking to surround myself with other ambitious people. If you're looking for a generalization, millennials are pretty ambitious. They want to help others and fulfill their vision for a better future. The stereotype of laziness stems from a lack of engagement, not a lack of ambition.

However, I must caution others. Ambition can be both a strength and weakness. At one point in my life, my ambition came at the cost of my happiness. Given, this was in the past, but it has taken me a long time to figure it out for myself.

I didn't want to listen to people who told me to be careful because "I could burn out." I used to think that burning out was a figment of our imaginations, but that's a lie.

The truth is that some millennials have very little ambition, but many are all the way at the other end of the spectrum. Most millennials want to be their own boss and change the world.

I *always* recommend that everyone (especially a millennial) should go for their wildest dreams. We can't ever let anyone take our dreams away from us. We must protect your dreams, we must cherish our dreams, and we must go to sleep every night dreaming of a better future. But, we also must take a moment and think about what our dreams are going to cost us.

Sacrifice is part of life. If we want something valuable, it's going to cost us time, money and energy to get it. There's no way around it.

When I was in college, I had started my own company and created the entrepreneurship club on campus. I was on top. I was a leader within the entrepreneurial ecosystem in Tallahassee, Florida, and I was a resource for students to start companies and change the world.

But secretly, I felt very lonely. My quality relationships were few and far between, and I really didn't have anyone to confide in. I didn't feel that any of my peers could relate to what I was going through. I was barely sleeping, and I was an emotional mess. I would use holiday breaks during college to catch up on work. When I went to de-stress at the end of the day, I would read articles, do research, and catch up on emails. These are things I associated with relaxation. There was a long period of time where I had no off switch. This is something I still struggle with today.

Instead of partying my face off like all my friends, I would stay up until 4 or 5 a.m. writing up proposals, marketing strategies, or even scheming my next business opportunity. I would wake up at 10 a.m., work until 10 p.m., work out, and then do the same thing all over again. I rationalized doing research and reading articles as productive, but that was far from the truth. It was my crutch.

I felt that working 18 hours a day made me better than other people. I felt that no one on the planet could keep up with me, but this ego boost came at the cost of my happiness.

If you work 18 hours a day, more power to you. I would never try to get in your way. I just challenge you to ask yourself if you're happy. Ask yourself if this is the life you dreamt of. If it's not, then you could also be experiencing the dark side of ambition.

To master success, happiness, fulfillment or whatever it is we want, we have to master our mindset. Becoming mindful of our current state, and the next action we must take is an art. What's best for us, and what's best for our business (or career) aren't always the same. Many of us may spend the rest of our lives battling the inner beast that's telling us to work 24/7/365. It's okay to obsess over your projects, but life is a constant balancing act. Real estate tycoon and sales training guru, Grant Cardone, recently wrote a book called *Be Obsessed or Be Average.* The best leaders of all time have been obsessed with their vision for a better future; it's one of the necessities of greatness.

However, overly ambitious people have the exact opposite problem that most people have. Instead of being lazy and unproductive, they overwork (1). Athletes face this problem all the time. If they want to be the best, they need to find the happy medium between productive growth, and overworking their muscles. Sometimes it's best to look at what will benefit you today, and other times, we must focus on what will benefit us tomorrow.

No matter what happens, we must make sure that we're not playing life on the edge of burnout. It's a path that only creates despair.

This chapter is here to serve as a warning. Ambition is both a blessing and a curse. I'm one of the most ambitious people you'll ever meet, and I must constantly keep myself in check to make sure I don't go overboard. My biggest fear in life is that I won't live up to my own expectations. There are many ambitious people out there who probably feel the same.

As you go throughout your life, you'll meet many people in this world who are filthy rich, but not happy. You'll also find many others who are filthy happy, but not rich. And then you'll find those people have just figured it out.

The Mental Shift Ambitious People Make in Their 20s. (2016, July 07). Retrieved December, 2016, from http://www.inc.com/empact/the-mental-shift-ambitious-people-make-in-their-20s.html

"Money is numbers, and numbers never end. If it takes money to be happy, your search for happiness will never end" – Bob Marley

◼ Fun

Fun is one of the best ways to hook millennial in to what you want. Fun can be found in the most obscure places. If you're not creating fun in the workplace, you're losing to your competitors who are. Ask yourself this question and be 100% honest.

"Are your employees suffering from terminal seriousness?"

Who ever said that maintaining professionalism means being serious all the time? I've walked into too many offices where there's not a smile in sight. The tension is so thick you can hear a pin drop. Is that the type of place you want to work in for 40 years? I don't think so.

What is life without fun? What is the point of life? Money? We already threw that one out the window. Most millennials would say happiness. And what's the root of happiness? FUN!

The world is a competitive place, and if your employees aren't having fun, they're going to find employment in a place they can. So, you might be asking yourself, "How the hell do I make the workplace fun? I work in a call center. Or an insurance agency. "But Jesse, there's no fun in insurance!"

I've worked in that industry and I'll tell you right now: if you believe that your industry (or company) is boring, it's going to rub off on all your employees (and eventually your customers). This is commonly referred to as projecting.

Children laugh on average 400 times a day (1). Some of these offices I've walked into would be lucky to get a handful of laughs all week. Laughter releases endorphins, a chemical in the brain 10X more powerful than morphine (2).

It's important to create a work environment that's relaxing. There are too many bad things happening in this world to take everything in life seriously. Sometimes it's best to just relax for a few minutes and throw a nerf ball around with a co-worker.

Now, I realize that your workplace is probably one where it's impossible to have fun. That's okay, I get it. But, if you were to try to implement some good times, here are a few things you could do to create fun in the workplace.

» Kick off your meetings with a funny story or even a You-Tube clip of a motivational speaker, or a comedian telling a joke.

» Celebrate holidays and people's birthdays. Don't just sweep them under the rug as "distractions" and "productivity killers."

» Bring in a speaker (or leader) from another company to engage the work force. Peak Performance workshops are literally my favorite thing to do in the world. It's important to make them engaging, informative and *fun*. It can add some spice in the workplace that employees aren't used to.

» Set aside one area of the office for relaxing or playing games. Most people create the association in their brain that the office means "work." If there's one place in the office that means "play," it'll allow the employees to find a mental escape when frustration sets in.

» Get a company pet. This could be a dog or cat. It could be a turtle. It could be a bearded dragon. Just make sure you're not imposing on anyone's allergies. There are reasons why some animals are used in therapy centers. They create emotional connections!

» Did someone say Karaoke? Although this is more fun after a few beers, it is an effective way to lighten the mood. Especially if the boss gets up there, loosens the tie, and lets the lead out.

» Speaking of a few beers, how about happy hour? You may not be the type to encourage drinking with co-workers, but what you should encourage are relationships with co-workers. If an employee wants to leave your company, they'll just leave. However, it will be a lot harder for them to let go if they love the people they work with. They may want to leave an employer, but they won't want to leave their friends.

» Decorate – you're spending a majority of your day there. Lighten the place up! Put up motivational pictures or quotes. A wall of expression. A funny meme. Who cares. Just make sure people will smile if they decide to look at the walls.

» How about a family lunch? Once in a while, take the whole team out to lunch. Or, order lunch in. Go watch a movie. Live a little. Sometimes the best ideas come when you're the most relaxed. It only takes one thought from one employee to change the whole company.

Stiff workplaces won't be around for much longer. They will lose to company cultures that promote good times. Fun goes along with spontaneity, so not everything you do has to be planned. You can wake up one morning and tell your employees you're taking a field trip to the aquarium. Why not? Your company won't fall apart from one afternoon trip. If it does, the field trip was the least of your worries.

Too many workplaces focus too much on "doing" and not enough on "being." You're working with people, not robots. Let them be themselves. Creative. Goofy. Sarcastic. Whatever it is. Let them be expressive, and the best version of themselves will shine.

With all that said, we're not looking to turn the workplace into a playground. Things still need to get done, and the company still needs to grow. However, in order for the company to grow, the individuals within the company must grow. It's a cause and effect.

Fun breaks up boredom and fatigue, it fulfils human social needs, it increases creativity, it improves communication, and it breaks up conflict (2). Fun can drastically impact your company culture and team morale. If you want to have a fun workplace, you need to focus on creating magical moments. This can be for employees or customers, spontaneous or planned. It really doesn't matter. Creating magic is an art and art is a creative process. So, get creative, have fun, and give your co-workers some positive emotions that they'll carry with them for the rest of their lives.

Urquhart, J. (n.d.). Creating a Fun Workplace... 13 Ways to Have Fun at Work! Retrieved January 06, 2017, from
http://www.agcareers.com/newsletters/creating.htm

Schwantes, M. (2016, July 08). These Simple Hacks Will Make You Super Creative, According to Science. Retrieved January, 2017, from _http://www.inc.com/marcel-schwantes/how-to-create-a-culture-of-super-creative-people-according-to-science.html_

■ Acceptance

Millennials must accept and acknowledge that there is so much of life we have not yet experienced. That knowledge will only come in good time, so there's no point in obsessing over it. We must accept what we cannot control. The truth is, most things in life we have absolutely no control over.

Here's a short list of things that used to frustrate me:

» Dishes

» Laundry

» Taxes

» Shopping for food and gas

» Weather

You'll notice that many of these are the inevitable vicious circles of life. These things are going to happen whether we like it or not. We can complain about them, or we can accept them. They are part of life. So, our best bet is to accept them and focus on the things we can control.

When I was at university, I learned a lesson from a friend (who wasn't the sharpest knife in the drawer). We were in the same business statistics class and happened to have a test the following day. The class was three tests; that's it. So, every test was a life or death situation.

The day before the test we had pulled an all-nighter studying. I wasn't a big statistics guy in college. Needless to say, I was freaking out. It was about 7:15 a.m. and we were sitting in the hallway doing our final review. My stress level was a 10 out of 10.

My friend looks at me with his typical blank stare and says, "Dude, you're a smart kid. Why do you get stressed out over shit you have no control over?" He stared at me and waited for a response, but I didn't have anything to say.

He was right. There was no point in stressing out. Whatever happened, happened. This test was not going to make or break my life. I wasn't going to fail out of college over one test. I was freaking out over something I had no control over.

I didn't have control over the questions. I didn't have control over my lack of preparation weeks ahead of time. That was all in the past. All I could focus on was the NOW. Right then, the only thing I could do was take a deep breath and relax.

So, instead of cramming information into my brain until 8 a.m., I went for a walk around campus and came back focused, and ready to crush it. I got a B on the test, and a B in the class.

After the test, I went up to my friend and expressed my gratitude for sharing that little piece of insight. He pretty much sat there and laughed in my face. He wasn't that kid who "gave advice," he just looked at it as common sense. It was, but not to me at that moment. I learned two very specific lessons that day.

1. I must accept the things in life that I have no control over.

2. I can learn things from anyone on the planet. Rich, poor, old, young, smart or stupid it doesn't matter. Everyone knows something that you don't.

I think there was a piece of me at one point in time that didn't want to admit that I didn't have control over everything. As an entrepreneur, I want to be in the driver's seat and take <u>total control</u> of my destiny. Accepting things, to me, was a sign of being mentally defeated by an outside force.

What I soon discovered was that both my friend and I were correct. There is a happy medium to acceptance. We have to accept what we can't control, but battle what we can. Millennials have accepted some of the social constructs that can't be changed today. However, this generation realizes that at some point, many of these transformations will be within our power. Eventually, we will stop accepting what was, and start changing the world to what will be.

Acceptance can be a slippery slope. It's very easy to just accept everything in life, which can put us in a state of complacency. Comfort is great for retired people, but part of becoming successful in business is about pushing ourselves outside of our comfort zone.

For the past 5 or 10 years, most people on this planet have lived in a state of acceptance. Accepting what's around them. Accepting what they make. Accepting negative relationships. Accepting mediocrity. And, accepting everything else in their life that's only okay.

Yes, we must accept things we have no control over, but when we do have a choice, we can't accept mediocrity. We all want to be outstanding. And, if we want to become outstanding, we must set high standards. If there's something in life we do have control over, we can't continue to accept average.

Most people live a mediocre life. They have mediocre relationships, with mediocre health, mediocre finances, and a mediocre job. They have all of this because their standards are just that – mediocre. The definition of mediocre itself is average. So, if you want to be above average, you must stop accepting what you *can* control, and start creating the extraordinary by taking the steering wheel of your life.

Other generations must accept what they can't control as well. If older generations spent as much time learning from millennials as they do criticizing them, companies with a multi-generational workforce would be in much better shape (1). Older generations need to accept our inadequacies because there's nothing they're going to be able to do to change them. Accept what you can't control, change what you can, and never forget that in this world, you only get what you tolerate.

Gimbel, T. (2016, May 03). Why It's a Good Idea to Invest in Millennials. Retrieved December, 2016, from http://www.inc.com/tom-gimbel/why-you-should-invest-in-millennials-.html

■ Expectations

The expectations of millennials and their elders are on two different wavelengths. Millennials expect to have a choice. Elders expect to have an obligation. Baby boomers had certain responsibilities, and they did whatever they had to do to fulfill their duties. Millennials believe that they can pick and choose how they spend their time.

Millennials want others to listen to our opinions before we give respect because we tend to believe that respect is earned, not given. However, boomers want to receive respect before they go and listen to a millennial's opinion. It's a double-edged sword. Both Millennials, and the generations that preceded them, want to be respected before they give respect. We must learn to merge our expectations to effectively collaborate in a multi-generational workforce.

Most of the problems in business (and in life) are a result of an expectation gap. Frequently expectation gaps occur when communication is not free-flowing. Expectations are important performance indicators within any organization. There should always be a KPI (Key Performance Indicator) for an employee, a team, and an organization as a whole. It's especially important that managers explain to millennials the KPI, and how to efficiently attain the result. There are many companies that don't let expectations become known until it's a problem. This is the worst time to bring expectations to light. The best way to avoid an expectation gap is to clearly and concisely communicate outcomes.

Organizations only get what they tolerate from both their employees and customers. Every business needs standards, and these standards will tell others what you will tolerate, and what you won't. Setting these expectations at the forefront is the best way to ensure peak performance across the entire company. Failure to set standards and expectations causes both communication and cultural discrepancies across organizations.

In one of my previous jobs, I had limited communication with my superiors. There was little face-to-face interaction, and the occasional phone call or email was the extent of our relationship. It was a concept I didn't know how to deal with at the time.

After three or four months, we had a team meeting on a Monday morning. My boss sent out an email saying how important it was that the whole team was dialed in for the conversation.

Once the phone call started, the boss-man spoke up and said something along the lines of, "Okay team, since some people are starting to struggle a little bit, what we're going to do is set some performance standards so that we're all on the same page."

He starts to go into a whole dialogue about what the new standards are, how they work, when we get a warning, and when we get fired. It was a pretty intense conversation, especially since half the team was obviously being targeted during the conversation. The standards just popped up out of nowhere – not only from a lack of performance, but also from the absence of an ongoing conversation.

Although I can appreciate the fact that the company iterated their process to better manage their employees, the way it was executed was subpar. I'm saying to myself, "This organization's been around for decades and *today* they're suddenly implementing standards?" I had a hard time understanding how the team had succeeded in previous years.

Standards and objectives should be set forth at the beginning of a relationship. It's important that a new hire understands exactly what's expected of them. How do you expect to keep a new hire on a track which they haven't been shown? If management wants that employee to grow and thrive, it's important that they set standards at the forefront and train them to exceed expectations. Once that happens, it's time to raise the bar – a great sign for any business.

Don't be the boss who lets their team run willy-nilly, then freak out on them when they're not performing. If you're saying, "Well shit, we don't have any standards (at least not ones that are communicated to the team). How do we just go about implementing standards?" The solution is easy.

Questions!

Ask the team for some feedback during a meeting. Come from a place of understanding and appreciating so that the standards being set are realistic and attainable. Ask them questions like:

» How long does it usually take to____?

» What's a realistic number of sales to have in a week / month?

» How often do you need to use____?

» When is the most appropriate time to have team meetings?

» How many prospects do you typically need to meet with to sell one unit?

» How much time should we typically spend on training each day?

» What is the one performance indicator we could use to determine progress within your role?

» What resources can we supply you with to help you better attain your outcomes?

This tactic is especially effective with millennials. By asking questions, managers can find out what their employees think are realistic standards. The key here is to <u>make the team a part of the process</u>. Employees may realize that there are complications, and that some things take longer than expected. That's perfectly fine. Standards can always adapt over time. By keeping the lines of communication open and creating ongoing conversations, the process can be perfected from the bottom up.

Our society needs to go through an expectation arbitration. If our generations work together, we can exceed everyone's expectations. But, if we don't merge ideologies, we'll never truly know what could have been.

▪ Flexibility

It's amazing what can happen when a degree of flexibility is given to a millennial. This could be something small like casual dress, or "half-day" Fridays during the summer. Or it could be something a little larger, like working from home for one or two days per week. It's not the flexible policy from management that makes the difference. It's the trust.

When we decide to trust millennials, something incredible happens. We're allowing that individual to tap into their creative potential, potential that can't be bought or purchased. The act of trust extends far beyond a casual dress code. It implies that we have faith in that person. It tells them that we care about their well-being just as much as the company's. It also may be one of the quickest ways to increase morale across the workplace. <u>Increased morale lowers attrition and absenteeism, which are two of the largest hidden costs in business</u>.

In the age of technology, tractability is second nature. There are many business people who work exclusively out of coffee shops like Starbucks. There are companies who have teams all over the globe, and use technology to connect and achieve a common goal.

Let's take working from home for example. When you allow a millennial to work from home a few days per week, the respect and trust will show that the company is committed to that person's well-being. It's a shift in thinking. Instead of working for us, that person is working with us. A partnership like this is more equitable for both parties.

Not only are we giving the employee a sense of freedom, but we're also tapping into a global talent pool. If an employee doesn't need to be in the office, do we really need to hire someone from our city? From our state? From our country? Maybe not.

I must say, nothing on this planet will ever replace a face to face meeting. However, with telecommuting technology, effective collaboration can be obtained. Working from home used to be considered an employee benefit, but an increasing number of companies are considering this part of their strategy. A strategic move like this could lead to easier employee acquisition and retention, which are two vital functions within an organization.

The reality is that some organizations can't function with a work-at-home model, and that's okay. The point here is to create a progressive culture that allows for flexibility. Not all employees function at their peak performance Monday to Friday, 9 a.m. to 5 p.m. I carry my projects 24/7 regardless of the time of day. Some of the best parts of this book have been written during my golden hours, 3-4 a.m. Would I expect my employees to do that? No. However, a good idea is a good idea, and if it comes to me in the middle of the night, I'm going to run with it.

Many of our elders would argue that millennials are flexible because of our age. We'll have to wait and see if we retain our flexibility as we get older. In the meantime, managers are going to have to become flexible with their employees. The name of the game for management is balance – what will make the customer happy, what will make the employee happy, and what will make the shareholders happy. Executives must be open and transparent with their team to engage them at the highest level and retain flexibility. Finding the happy medium will require communication, which is a two-way street (in case we forgot). If we iterate the flexibility within the office, we'll be sure to come up with the optimal strategy that will help our organization thrive in this modern world.

A tree
with strong
roots laughs
at storms.
~Malay Proverb

How We Work

■ Work / Life Integration

O ur fixation on flexibility has created a paradigm shift in work-life balance. There is a huge misconception that this generation simply has a poor work ethic. However, if we dig deeper, that poor work ethic can be attributed to a lack of engagement, not a lack of persistence.

If millennials want something, then trust that they will have the fortitude to make it happen. There are talkers and doers in every generation, and only time will uncover the true millennial champions. To say that we're weak because we quit jobs we don't like is short-sighted. Based on some of our other values, it's apparent that millennials are just on the search for an awesome work experience that will add value to both their personal and professional lives.

You see, there's really no such thing as a work-life balance. There's just life. The dichotomy between work and life is a lie because work never truly ends. If someone makes their whole life their work, then there's no time for them to live the life they've always desired. Unfortunately, what happens is that we end up living the life we're told to live. Millennials don't want to go from day to day managing their life; they want to design a life. Designing a life includes things like family, friends, fitness, and *fun*, along with finances. Again, if you're not creating a fun workplace for your employees, they will run off to an employer who does.

Many people think that millennials wanting a work-life balance means that they really don't want to work. That couldn't be further from the truth. Millennials work on a 24/7 schedule, anywhere in the world, however they need to. That's the new way.

Desks and offices can be nice, but they aren't a necessity for millennials. We don't need to be in the office 9 a.m. to 5 p.m., Monday to Friday. If that's the company policy, check to see how many people are at their desks at 5:05 p.m. on any given day.

Then, do a little experiment and change the policy to "make sure the work is done." Check the office at 5:05 p.m. a few weeks later and see what the difference is. Many managers may be surprised to find employees working away and enjoying the process.

To millennials, rules are made to be broken. If there is a policy that says someone must work until 5 p.m., the countdown starts at 4 p.m. If management says, "Hey, we need to get these things done by the end of next week. Let's have a meeting Monday morning to make sure we're all on the same page," management may see a millennial there at 7 p.m. on a Friday. Millennials are more than willing to work in a Starbucks on Sunday afternoon, and many of us are willing to take a phone call at 10:00 at night. However, if the company policy is 9 a.m. to 5 p.m. you better believe that your employees will be out the door by 5:01. If you don't believe me, go look at a millennial's Snapchat story on any given day at 4 p.m. The countdown has begun.

Instead of work-life balance, maybe we should be having a conversation about work-life integration. There are 168 hours in a week and 40 of those hours are (typically) spent working.

This means that we work 23.8% of the week, and the rest of the time is ours. But, for some reason we're stuck in the social construct that the ~24% of the week we spend working is right smack dab in the middle of the best hours! The 24% starts to feel more like 50% when we're commuting and spending our nights answering emails.

One of the big four accounting firms, Deloitte, did a millennial study that found that most millennials think the balance between work and life is more vital than financial compensation (1). Time is the new money. Time is our most valuable asset, and time is the one thing in our lives that only moves in one direction. It's our only resource that's non-refundable.

All of the older generations seemed to separate their work from their fun. However, millennials want their work to be fun. It sounds pretty obvious which one is the better choice. We watched our baby boomer parents delay happiness in return for career advancement (2). We've learned from their experience, and seek an atmosphere that will promote professional development, happiness, and growth.

Millennials grew up watching baby boomers and Generation X burn out. They worked overtime and they hustled. No one can knock them for that. They had a work ethic that was unprecedented in the 20th century. However, if we stopped any of those people working overtime and asked them how their life was, they would have most likely told us "it sucked" or more commonly, "I did what I had to do to support my family and get by."

If you must make ends meet, you either hustle or you die. There's no way around it. But, if you're not fighting to put food on your table, there's no reason why you can't integrate your work with everything else you do in life.

Our parents failed when it came to work-life integration. Many of them didn't have a choice at the time. They did what they needed to do to provide for their family, and my hat goes off to them. I have the highest sense of respect for their dedication and work ethic.

Today is a different story. If a millennial knows the outcome they're going after, it's their responsibility to make sure it happens. They're responsible for a certain result, and if they don't attain those results, shorten the leash, or have an open and honest conversation about it. If the problem persists, fire them! If they want work-life integration, but can't handle it, they can go waste someone else's time, money and energy. Work-life integration requires discipline. And, discipline is something that employees either have or they don't. Work-life integration requires employees to be dedicated to their results. If they can't do that, then they don't deserve the freedom.

If that millennial has satisfactory performance and discipline, feel free to give them the autonomy they deserve. Work-life integration is a trial and error process, and every employee is a little different. Much like iterative design, it's important to test different strategies with different people. Just remember, people have a life outside their cubical, and if management respects that, employees will be more grateful, appreciative, and productive moving forward.

The 2016 Deloitte Millennial Survey. (2016). Retrieved from
https://www2.deloitte.com/content/dam/Deloitte/global/Documents/About-Deloitte/gx-millenial-survey-2016-exec-summary.pdf

Solomon, M. (2016, January 27). You've Got Millennial Employees All Wrong; Here Are The Four

Things You Need To Know Now. Retrieved January, 2017, from

http://www.forbes.com/sites/micahsolomon/2016 /01/26/everything-youve-heard-about-millennial- employees-is-baloney-heres-the-truth-and-how-to-use- it/#45e22fb254ee

■ Turnover and Attrition

There are lots of people leaving their jobs, which means there are tons' millennials looking to engage in meaningful work!

Many millennials will leave their job in the next two years. Many of them may be at your companies. However, many of them may also be at your competitor's companies, and those people could be your largest future assets. There are reasons why millennials are leaving their jobs, and it's not because we're lazy, entitled brats. <u>No matter how great technology gets, quality leadership and human capital will always be in demand</u>.

If you're turning over a bunch of employees, there could be a whole laundry list of problems. Here are some of the most common reasons why companies have a hard time retaining millennials:

» Conflict of values.

» No work-life integration.

» No connection to the company purpose or bigger picture.

» No upward mobility or leadership opportunities.

» Mediocre training and development (both personal and professional).

» Lack of empathy from both management and customers.

» Their expectations were not met (large expectation gap).

» Emotional blocks and inner conflicts between any two employees.

» No legitimate forms of motivation – no activities to engage and empower the employee.

» Feeling undervalued, unappreciated, and not heard by management.

» Lack of transparency and feedback.

» Inadequate systems and policies that cause frustration.

» No vision, or a constantly changing vision.

» No fun zone.

» Management only encourages employees to do, not think. <u>Turnover and attrition are the largest hidden costs in any business with employees</u>. It's a lot easier to retain and properly train an employee than it is to go through multiple people each year. The hiring process will cost you time, money and energy – and training will do the same. Focus on finding outstanding employees and properly engaging them. It'll allow you to use your resources to grow, not just to stay alive.

Some of the hidden costs involved in turnover include: exit costs, recruiting, interviewing, hiring, orientation, training, compensation and benefits while training, lost productivity, customer dissatisfaction, lost (or reduced) business, administrative costs and most importantly, lost expertise (1). I've consulted with companies who have high turnover rates and claim "that's just part of the business." Very infrequently do they look within their company culture or management team to decrease the number of short term employees. Across jobs, the cost of replacing an employee is clustered between 10% and 30% of an employee's annual salary (with an average of 20%) (2).

Is the lack of millennial tenure a result of laziness and entitlement? Or is it a result of a global culture shift that companies have a hard time identifying with? I'd say it's a combination of the two. If you're thinking, "There's nothing I can do to keep millennials engaged and productive in the office," then you're right; but only because you believe so. Playing the victim card, sitting there and pouting, and watching your business fall to the ground sound like reasonable outcomes for someone not willing to adapt to multi-generational tactics. Or, you can suck it up and realize that in the 21st century, change is not a should item on the to-do list – it's a must item.

All these millennials that are quitting their jobs are not quitting because they're bad employees (although inevitably, some of them are). They're quitting because they're not engaged at the highest level, and they know there's an opportunity out there that will allow them to tap into more of their potential.

It's time to make sure our businesses are focusing on employees, customers, and the community that surrounds them. Offerings will come and go, so we're really looking to build a corporate culture that will outlast any of our products or services. Cultures are built around people, and people rally behind a purpose. Make sure your business is serving a legitimate purpose so that millennials will feel like they're contributing something to the greater good of society. If you do this, the right employees will stay and the wrong ones will go.

The Hidden, Deadly Costs of Employee Turnover. (n.d.). Retrieved January, 2017, from http://www.hri-online.com/blog/the-hidden-deadly-costs-of-employee-turnover

Boushey, H., & Glynn, S. (2012, November 16). There Are Significant Business Costs to Replacing Employees. Retrieved January, 2017, from https://www.americanprogress.org/issues/economy/reports/2012/11/16/44464/there-are-significant-business-costs-to-replacing-employees/

CUSTOMERS WILL NEVER LOVE YOUR COMPANY UNTIL THE EMPLOYEES LOVE IT FIRST.

- SIMON SINEK -

∎ Upward Mobility

Here's the sad reality: most people take a job and have absolutely no clue where the next step is in their professional life. It's a blind bet. They go all in with hopes that it works out, and then six months later, they leave, and management's scratching their heads and asking themselves, "Why?"

If millennial retention is a top priority, then corporations need to show their employees how they will grow both personally and professionally during their tenure with the organization. Does that mean the company needs to continuously give their employees incentives? Yes – yes it does.

Traditionally, it has always been thought that corporate incentives have to do with money, but this generation is proving that philosophy wrong. We know that this generation values traveling and gaining experience. So maybe a good incentive would be to send a millennial to a conference for a week, completely paid for by the company. Upward mobility doesn't always involve an upgrade in position. Upward mobility is any type of incentive that promotes growth within an employee.

You may think that conferences (and other forms of "fluff") are a waste of time, money, and energy. But, that perspective does not consider a more holistic and growth oriented approach to upward mobility. Every company needs to create an upward mobility vision that employees can attach themselves to. One of the best millennial retention strategies is to constantly feed growth opportunities to those who seek it.

It's important to show your employees how they can advance their lives both inside and outside the company. Show them exactly what needs to get done and the expectations in doing so. Keeping the lines of transparency open when discussing upward mobility is crucial.

As we spoke about, in corporate America, there's a little term called "skipping the line." Some would consider it cheating, and those who do are most likely the people who have had to methodically climb the ranks of their organization. The people who are keen on jumping the line realize that tenure and role advancement are not mutually exclusive. Unfortunately, the reality is that someone may be ready for promotion, but they can't move easily because a suitable position is not available, or it is blocked by someone in it who is not going to move anytime soon (1).

When I say, "jump the line," I'm talking about taking a short-cut or the fast track to success. Employees typically jump the line within a company by exceeding expectations. The more traditional way to jump the line may involve a new employment opportunity with a competitor. Now, in the general sense of the term, success doesn't have any short cuts. Some people get there quickly; others take the long route. But, all successful people put one foot in front of the other and overcome the obstacles handed to them.

We must work smart and hard to attain our deepest desires. Success and growth are systematic changes developed through awareness and iteration. The more you try, the more you'll fail. The more you fail, the more opportunity you'll find to succeed.

Millennials tend to think that how things have always been done in corporate America is boring. Doing things in a new innovative way is stimulating to both the individual and the company. It's not that we want to be rebellious; we just realize that the age of technology has brought about new opportunities that need to be taken advantage of. Technology provides a world full of smart cuts, and opportunities to systematize processes. A lack of responsiveness from management to changing times can stagnate both upward mobility and corporate growth. Unfortunately, like lots of things in life, sometimes as a millennial, shutting your mouth is your best bet. Being right doesn't matter if it comes at the cost of employment. There's a fine line between offering constructive insight, and over stepping your boundaries. A millennial's best bet is to let out the line little by little as they build more rapport with their superiors.

If you happen to be an entrepreneur, upward mobility is a road you must travel alone. However, don't look at this as a pit fall. This gives people the opportunity to completely write their own story. If we're employed, part of our story is written for us. As an entrepreneur, we have the opportunity to create our own upward mobility staircase to success. We can skip the line, cut the tape, and scream out to the guy in the front of the line – no one's really stopping us.

Just remember, *how* we get there is just as important as the destination itself. We don't want to be remembered as the slime ball that had to stab a few backs to get where we need to be. We can never go wrong by doing things ethically and methodically.

Even executives need to have an upward mobility path so they can see how they can have more responsibility, more impact and most likely, more money. Upward mobility isn't necessarily about job titles – it's about growth over time.

Millennials are looking to build a foundation of stepping stones as we build our personal success staircase. Would working a couple of Saturdays per month get us where we want to go quicker? Most likely. There are professionals across the world that find a way to take the elevator to success, instead of the stairs. <u>However, elevators are built by other people. The stairs are built by you</u>. Elevators are major leverage, and major leverage occurs through relationships with the right people. Whether you're an employee, or an entrepreneur, it's important that you begin to paint your vision for your upward mobility journey. <u>Everyone on this planet is one handshake away from their big break</u>. Our relationships can make or break our careers. It's a process that can take decades. All we need to do today is focus on the next step in front of us.

We live in a time where anyone can decide when they will become successful. We have empowered ourselves to be in control of our advancements, both within corporate America and outside of it. We must always remember that there's no short cut to success. But, the one thing that will significantly increase the speed of our journey is meeting the right people.

Deal, J., & Levenson, A. (2016, January 21). Training Journal. Retrieved January, 2017, from https://www.trainingjournal.com/articles/feature/millennials-are-ambitious-and-crave-career-progression

■ The Two Division Company

The two-division company methodology breaks down the invisible walls within organizations. If properly implemented, processes are streamlined and communication flows freely. These two improvements are exactly what this generation wants; and if the improvements are good for millennials, they're good for business.

Tech gurus may negate this concept, but it's a fact of business.

There are only two divisions within a company.

1. There's a sales division, which includes all the roles that generate direct revenue for the company.

2. There's a sales support division, which is every other function within business that doesn't produce revenue. This is the foundation for the sales division to thrive upon.

Tech companies (especially startups) get all caught up in the user base because many of them are pre-revenue. Although I don't like that business model in particular, the people within the company who spend time on activities to acquire their user base would be considered the sales team. This assumes that the user base will eventually turn into paid customers.

This two-division structure keeps an organization as flat as possible. Too many companies focus on building up, as opposed to out. However, building up is a recipe for disaster, especially in the beginning. What every company needs are more people selling, and more people supporting those sales people. Anyone that's in the middle is corporate fat. And in business, it's always appropriate to cut the fat. Strong businesses run lean because they have muscle, and muscle is created through the patterns, habits, and systems that are implemented within the organization. It takes discipline to go to the gym and build muscle, just like it does in business. Cutting the fat is cutting out all the activities that are not driving the company forward.

This keeps everyone's scope of work in either money-making activities, or direct support of those money-making activities. This is a model I learned from Michael Houlihan, the founder of Barefoot Wines. He used this concept while developing his company before selling to Gallo Wines in 2005. He had an ingenious way of enforcing the two-division company concept. His 401K matching program was based on quarterly growth, sales, and profitability. This helped ensure that everyone was driven toward the same result.

The Sales Team

While speaking with Michael, I got some insight as to how complicated his sales process was. He told me that there were seven sales that had to be made throughout the value chain in order to make sure the customer cracked open a bottle of Barefoot Wine.

1. <u>Management</u> must sell <u>their own staff</u> on the company mission.

2. <u>Sales people</u> must sell <u>the distributor</u> on why they should warehouse Barefoot Wine for strategic reasons.

3. Sales people must sell the distributors' sales manager on how Barefoot Wine will help the distributor achieve their sales goals.

4. Sales people must sell the distributors' sales people on how to sell to the retailers and maximize their own commissions on a regular basis.

5. Sales people must sell the distributors' retail buyers on how Barefoot Wine will drive foot traffic in store.

6. Sales people must sell the retail buyers' managers and clerks on how to sell Barefoot Wine to their consumers.

7. Sales people must sell the general public on why Barefoot Wine is the best bang for their buck.

Every sale that had to be made was structured differently based on the beliefs and values of that specific counterpart. Every part of the distribution chain must be sold on the best way to maximize value. Suddenly, I began to realize that this multifaceted sales process had a ton of moving parts (that could all go wrong). One break in the chain causes profits to drain from the sales pipeline. Getting the distributor to sell to the store, and getting the store employee to sell to the customer are two completely different types of sales.

The Sales Support Team

This is every single function of the company that doesn't directly produce money. This includes, but is not limited to: management, accounting, operations, customer support, human resources, research and development, etc.

You may be wondering, "How does this apply to millennials?" This business practice helps to streamline communication and scope of work. Creating these efficiencies will help a millennial thrive and tap into more of their potential. This is a way of running a company that's fairly unique in modern business.

However, what this construct does is simplify a company's scope. Too many companies focus on a scope of work that's defined by employment sites. A given job description may have 17 activities and responsibilities, and 6 qualifications. But, if we play to our employees' strengths, every individual (regardless of their title) is performing tasks they're outstanding at. No one cares about cookie-cutter job descriptions; they're a waste of time. Customizing the scopes of work will help to grow dynamic teams. This business structure is effective for millennials because it clarifies and simplifies the flow of information, and allows the scope of work for each employee to be based off that individual's strengths.

The executives at Barefoot Wines sat down with their employees and let them choose their own scope of work. Suddenly, activities were getting done that weren't on the radar previously. When you give millennials the autonomy to accomplish their outcomes based on their strengths, innovation takes place and achievers thrive.

■ Policy

Company policy is a bit tricky these days. This new generation likes stirring the pot. It's akin to the U.S. Constitution. Is what was written hundreds of years ago directly applicable today? Well, yes and no. It's a little more complicated than that.

The bottom line is that everyone (especially management) must always be looking to improve their company in any way possible. Organizational policy is just one of those constant and never ending improvements.

Policy walks a fine line, and it's something that can have a dramatic impact on a company's culture. Managers don't want to create bureaucratic bullshit, but at the same time, they don't want employees running wild. There needs to be some happy medium.

Keeping a company policy the same just because "that's how it's always been" is a constricting ideology. That's playing your cards safe; and in today's world, safe is a losing strategy. When people play safe, they always end up sticking to what they know – the current policy. The same mindset holds true for consumers making purchasing decisions. When consumers face uncertainty, they tend to stick to what they know (which doesn't involve purchasing your product).

Remember, what "was," what "is," and what's "going to be" are three completely different stories. If they're not, your company is never going to expand to its fullest capability. It will only ever be what was, and that's a recipe for disaster (especially with this generation).

We're living in a world where "what was" is just plain old boring. It's not that "what was" isn't good. It's just that "what was" can be improved, and "what was" may not be as applicable in 21st century business. The past is most applicable when it's being used to create the future.

Creating and developing policy walks a fine line between "what's in the best interest of the shareholders," "what's in the best interest of the employee," and "what's in the best interest of the customer." Sometimes what's in the best interest of the customer, employee and company result in completely different outcomes. It's about finding that happy medium and creating a company culture where policies can be iterated if they aren't fitting well. Creating a culture where policies benefit the customers, the employees, and the shareholders will always be a winning strategy. Unfortunately, finding a policy like that is easier said than done.

A common example of a flawed policy is "No social media at work." Let me put it frankly. If employees are looking for a distraction, and managers tell them that they can't use social media, employees are just going to find a different distraction. Creating a social media policy isn't going to stop millennials from getting distracted or disengaged. It's just going to cause employees to get resentful that management's policies don't empower their workforce. According to a PwC report, millennials expect the technologies that empower their personal lives to also drive communication and innovation in the workplace (1).

Saying employees can't use social media in the workplace is telling them that their discretion is not trusted. Inadvertently, management is telling them that they are "wasting time," and "not partaking in activities that drive the company forward." But, management must remember that micromanaging, and causing employees unneeded stress, may do more harm than checking Facebook at the water cooler. Companies such as IBM and ADP have met this need by developing workplace technology systems that promote real-time, ongoing dialogue across all employment levels. Tools like Yammer, Jive, Chatter, and slack (along with social networks) are helping employees collaborate across functional and geographic boundaries (2).

Can an open social media policy bring a company down? Absolutely. It's about learning, iterating and firing the employees who abuse an open policy. When benchmarking company policies, the best thing you can do is open the conversation to the group. The millennials within the group will appreciate you so much more for doing so. Who knows? You may discover a policy that can catalyze your company's growth.

Millennials at work Reshaping the workplace. (n.d.).
Retrieved   January,   2017,   from
https://www.pwc.com/m1/en/services/consulting/do
cuments/millennials-at-work.pdf

Benson,   T.   (2016,   February   11).   Motivating
Millennials Takes More than Flexible Work Policies.
Retrieved   January,   2017,   from
https://hbr.org/2016/02/motivating-millennials-takes-
more-than-flexible-work-policies

Managing

Millennials don't want bosses; they want coaches. This is a fundamental shift in thinking and managers need to get with it. Millennials are not looking for someone to hold our hand, command us, and control us. Today's management needs to look more like a coaching and facilitating process.

Here's a statement a typical boss would have made in the 20th century followed by a question. "Hey, I noticed your numbers fell last week; is there anything you want to talk about?" There are so many things wrong with this statement. No one wants to talk about what's wrong, so this is a loaded question.

Here's an improved version of the same statement. "Hey, I noticed last week was a little slower for you. What can I do to better support you? Is there anything I can do to help you?" This opens the door up for a conversation. You can follow up with questions like, "What's the one thing you need to improve on this week to get back on target?" or "When should we revisit this conversation to make sure we're on the same page? I'll follow up in 48 hours – does that work for you?"

It's about assimilating to the millennial and letting them know that you're on the same team. Too often managers position themselves as superiors. Although we can appreciate having a sense of hierarchy, there needs to be a culture of equality within the work place. We all work at this company and we're working together to achieve a certain outcome. It just so happens that as a manager; your job is to facilitate growth and do whatever it takes to get your team to the next level.

Many problems typically arise from new managers, both hired and promoted. They feel that it's their job to assert themselves in this new-found role. However, instead of focusing on asserting themselves as an authority, new managers should focus on a benchmarking process.

To improve, managers must fully understand where their subordinates are at today. Here are some solid methodologies for benchmarking both individual and company progress and performance:

» Have each employee fill out a short accountability form once a week.

» Hold open office hours once a week where any employee can come speak to you about any issues they're having.

» Put an anonymous suggestion box in the office, read the notes privately, gather your thoughts and then speak about the suggestions publicly to gain more feedback.

» Publicly commend top performers, most improved, and hard workers. Talk about what they did, how they did it, and how others can emulate their success.

It's important to realize that benchmarking is pointless if the organization doesn't have effective growth strategies. Implementing companywide change isn't always feasible for a manager. Here are a few simple strategies any manager can use to help grow a millennial employee:

» Create incremental outcomes. Pushing them a little further each week is huge. During your ongoing conversations, you'll be able to show progress in the numbers. It'll make them want to stick around for years to come.

» Give out random gifts to top performers and people improving. Don't make this a generic activity. Give something different to employees based on their interests. Show them that you care, and most importantly, that you've been listening.

» Give employees who are performing well a little slack. If they want to come in an hour later, and stay an hour later, go for it. Find ways to progressively show that you trust subordinates. It's important to allow employees to earn the little perks over time.

» Have a go-to company book. Maybe it's this one; maybe it's not. Most importantly, have a guide book that you can reference in meetings that outlines ideologies that align with the organization's vision and mission.

» Look to understand how an employee's personal life is affecting their work. Our lives are interconnected works of art. Frustration in the workplace could have to do with an employee's relationships, health, spirituality, mindset, etc. Managers can benefit from taking a more holistic view of the situation by becoming mindful of the fact that workplace problems are not always workplace related.

None of these things matter if the organization is not hiring effective leaders. I'm not keen on the word management because managing is more of a guiding and facilitating process today. Managers have a tough job, especially with millennials. I never said that we are easy to deal with. That couldn't be further from the truth!

Millennials tend to question everything – I'm guilty of it myself. We don't mean it in a disrespectful way. All we want to do is to understand. To gain compliance from millennials, we need to give the rationale behind our instructions (1). Once we understand why something is the way it is, we can come to terms with the request, or start finding more efficient ways to accomplish the same outcomes. Sometimes as a manager, listening is the best thing we can do.

With that said, millennials need to be conscientious of the fact that it's not always appropriate to ask questions. There's a fine line between trying to understand something, and undermining someone's authority.

Millennials are looking for leaders (and companies) that will help them develop their specific strengths. We know that by using our strengths, we have infinite potential. It seems like when we go and speak to a boss, though, all we hear about is what *isn't* possible. We hear about all the limits, restrictions and confines set upon our role, company, industry or society. No one, especially millennials, wants to hear about what isn't possible.

Do not put ceilings on your employee's potential. Does that mean throw out company policies and rules? No, we're not looking to create another *Lord of the Flies.* We're looking to destroy limitations.

As humans, our potential is unlimited. But, if we're constantly hearing what we can't do, then we'll only ever be okay. As a manager, it's your job to paint millennials a picture of all the possibilities. Don't tell us what isn't possible. Tell us what is. Tell us that with hard work and dedication, we can achieve anything we set our minds to. Tell us that you will be there with us every step of the way. And most importantly, tell us that the only limits in this world, are the ones we set on ourselves. Because that, my friends, is the truth.

Taylor, K. (n.d.). The Tethered Generation. Retrieved January, 2017, from http://holycrossenergyleadershipacademy.com/uploads/Tethered_Generation_Motivation_-_Tyler.pdf

TRUE LEADERS
DON'T CREATE
FOLLOWERS,
THEY CREATE
MORE LEADERS

■ Leading and Mentoring

No technology will ever replace quality leadership. It will always be in demand, and is the root of all progress within our society. Progress comes from momentum and leaders create momentum. If millennials are going to become the leaders of tomorrow, it's imperative that they are given the proper guidance today.

When there is no leadership, failure is soon to follow. Whether it's in business or in life, bad leadership is followed by evil. When leadership has no integrity, it has no authority. And when it has no authority, hatred ensues. Most followers are looking for leaders with integrity and authority. Every single problem we've ever encountered on this planet can be solved by a great leader. Maybe that great leader is you.

We need righteous, conscientious and charismatic leaders now more than ever. There are too many people in this world that are waiting until they're in positions of power to become leaders. <u>Leadership is not a role, it's an action</u>. Leadership is not something you have; it's something you do. If you want to be a great leader, start taking actions to move in that direction.

Great leaders serve as mentors to their followers. Whether you're leading a company, a country, or an ideology, all your supporters are looking to you to guide them in the right direction. However, being a great leader doesn't necessarily mean knowing all the ins and outs of the business. Many leaders rely on the knowledge of their followers and their team for progress. Great leaders don't always have all the answers. Great leaders embrace collaborative environments (1).

Millennials are the leaders of tomorrow and in order for them to become trailblazers of the future, they need proper mentorship. Here are a few mentoring techniques to help leaders further develop over time:

» Virtual mentoring – This is all about resourcefulness. There are thought leaders all over the web. Find two to three that you like and watch their videos, read their content and engage with them. You can still be led by people you never have (or will never) meet. Leverage the power of the internet.

» Self-mentoring – This is all about self-awareness. If you don't have a current mentor (like I did for many years), mentor yourself. Reflect on your thoughts, emotions, and actions, and write things down. At the end of the day, if you can't lead yourself, how can you expect to lead others? This is an activity everyone should go through.

» Group mentoring – This is all about collaboration. The manager, executive, or leader facilitates the growth process and asks thought-provoking questions to move the group's conversation forward. This takes very few resources and can help the team grow as a whole.

» Detached mentoring – This is all about objectivity. This mentor is outside the organization and has a third-party perspective on situations. These conversations can usually be more open and personal since there's no conflict of interest.

» Situational mentoring – This is all about circumstance. Whichever problem you're currently having, find a thought leader in that space and soak up their knowledge. Learn their ways, then move on to the next problem that needs solving. The right mentor at the right time can make a huge impact. This uses the concept of just-in-time learning.

» Reverse mentoring – This is all about listening. Pair a millennial with an executive or manager, but let the younger person do the mentoring. This coaching process will give the millennial confidence, and the executive a chance to learn valuable lessons he would have never learned otherwise. This process could also lead into a co-mentoring relationship where coaching flows both ways.

» Formal mentoring – The most traditional form of mentoring is typically referred to as managing or leading. If you're reading this book, you probably mentor more people than you realize. Mentoring involves listening carefully and asking great questions.

Having a mentor gives a millennial mental security. It lets them know that if they're frustrated in the workplace, they have someone outside the situation looking out for them. Every millennial wants to grow more, do more, achieve more, and have more – and all of that starts with the ability to learn and openly communicate. There is a major difference between helping someone with their job, and helping someone with their life. If you want to be a great mentor, both are necessary to really take someone to the next level.

The technology age has allowed leaders to find new followers and followers to find new leaders. Millennials have given light to a modern age of leadership, one where a single video or text can turn you from a puppet to a puppeteer, or from a follower to an influencer. However, no matter how great technology gets, quality leaders will always be in demand. Let's just hope that as our society moves forward, we put the right leaders in the right seats. The alternative could be devastating.

Marketing, O. (2014, October 30). Three Things Everyone Should Know About Millennial Leaders. Retrieved January, 2017 , from http://www.forbes.com/sites/onmarketing/2014/10/29/three-things-everyone-should-know-about-millennial-leaders/2/#262a0dc043f6

■ The Team

There is nothing more important in business than the team that provides the foundation for an organization. Without a strong team, individuals perish. With a strong team, individuals support and enable their peers' growth. Groups create support systems and means for constantly finding ways to improve processes within the company.

When functioning within a team, it's important that individuals have a sense of autonomy over their actions. When a millennial gets promoted from sales rep to sales manager, it doesn't mean their independence should be taken away.

Will there always be certain tasks that a manager must do? Absolutely, and managers (especially new hires) should be held accountable for the scope of work deemed appropriate. However, companies should empower them to achieve in the way that facilitates their own personal growth. If a millennial is confined to strict corporate procedures, there's no way for that person to express themselves creatively. If the company is looking for cogs in a wheel, they should look for a different type of employee.

Teams tend to know each other on a professional level, but fail to connect on a personal level. It's important to connect with the team from an emotional standpoint to create a cohesive unit. It doesn't matter whether you're a peer or superior. Looking for ways to connect and develop the team will always benefit the organization.

Strengthening the team is strengthening the company, and sometimes the best way to do that is to strengthen the ties within the team. At the end of the day, if an employee wants to leave the company, they'll leave. If they want to leave the company and don't leave, they'll become toxic to the team. They'll be poisonous, unproductive, and cause viral disengagement across the whole team. If they want to go, but aren't telling management, then it's your job to figure it out and get them out of the door ASAP. Failing to do so will continue to cost the organization valuable resources.

However, if an employee struggling within their role really likes the people they're working with, they'll find a way to make it work. They'll stay not because they love the company so much, but because they love their coworkers. If they're attached to the team, perfect! Now all management needs to do is help them thrive within their specific role.

It's important to keep the lines of communication wide open on a multi-generational team. Over-communication is always better than insufficient communication (1). Let people work collaboratively on a project. Conquer and divide is always a winning strategy. If they want to, let them work autonomously on a project and then bounce ideas off their peers. Teams can be thought of as mini families (or tribes) within the organization. Making the team dynamic flat (as opposed to hierarchical) will help make everyone feel that their contribution is valued (1).

I've seen a new trend where team leaders (managers) are allowing teams to name themselves, develop their own logos, and create their own cultures within the organization. I think this is a great idea! It's very easy for employees to feel lost and undervalued at large corporations. If we let individuals feel that they're a part of a tribe within the greater company vision, we're setting them up for long term success.

The team is about more than collaboration. It's about love. Great teams function like families. If you watch any great team work together, it literally looks like a dance. Whether it's a business, sports team, orchestra, or marriage, all outstanding teams communicate openly and honestly.

Getting a bunch of individualist millennials to move in one direction is easier than you would think. If your company has good leadership, and is driven by a purpose, the right employees will stick. Attrition is inevitable (to a certain extent). However, in all reality, you want the bad apples to fall from the tree and the good ones to stick around. The fate of your business lies within the successes, failures, and strengthening of the communication on your team.

Koloc, N. (2016, March 08). Why Baby Boomers and Millennials Make Great Teams. Retrieved January, 2017, from http://99u.com/articles/14709/why-baby-boomers-and-millennials-make-great-teams

■ Collaboration

I f there's one positive thing you can say about this generation, it's that our sense of community (both globally and locally) is at an all-time high. Millennials realize that together we are so much more powerful than we are as individuals.

Collaboration is a way to create a mastermind, a third mind that's infinitely more powerful than the sum of its parts. Therefore technology communication platforms like Slack, Messenger, and WeChat, as well as project management platforms like, Asana and Basecamp, have taken off. Collaboration is not about taking individual credit for every single little thing. It's about starting a discussion where everyone on the team can create together. Many companies compartmentalize functions within the organization. However, promoting cross-pollination allows companies to get a greater diversity of ideas by collaborating with a greater diversity of creative people – people from a variety of disciplines, departments, cultures, ages, mindsets, motivations, and orientations (1).

This touches slightly on the concept of transparency and interconnectedness. Asking your employees how you can do better is one of the most empowering ways to get and receive collaborative feedback. It's communicating to the other party that you're always looking to improve – an important facet of 21st century business.

Showing this progressiveness is a great way to align with a millennial. Collaborating with employees (whether they are above or below you) is a great way to create a sense of empathy.

Our generation was brought up in an atmosphere predicated on equal relationships. Our parents, our teachers, and our bosses work with us to come up with a solution. Collaboration is all about creating a co-decision-making process, as opposed to an authoritative figure just demanding us to "do this."

The hardest part of collaboration can be constructive criticism. We all say, "no ideas are bad ideas," but when push comes to shove, there is only one idea that gets implemented. Inevitably, all the other ideas get thrown away or put on the back burner. This means employees must assess ideas based on the benefits to the company, not the individual.

There are many communication techniques to ease this conversation, but the most popular one tends to be the compliment sandwich. Here's how it works (2):

» **Compliment**: show the individual how they helped the group perspective.

» **Constructive criticism**: tell them why their idea wasn't the best option for the team, and how they can improve by implementing certain changes.

» **Compliment**: show them how their perspective is valuable in creating changes within the company moving forward.

Collaboration is a progressive ideology. Many companies think they collaborate just because they have a white board wall. It's a bit more complicated than that. It comes down to the core of the company, and needs to be ingrained culturally to work efficiently. Collaboration is more than an activity. It's a way of thinking, and a way for millennials to further understand the perspectives of their counterparts. Open team collaboration is the solution to many organizational problems faced in corporate America. Collaboration isn't something that's written in your operations manual, or company mission. It's a type of instinctive action that's a part of a company's ideology. By collaborating, you're reiterating that teams working together are infinitely more valuable than the sum of their parts.

Cross Pollination: How and Why It Works. (n.d.). Retrieved January, 2017, from https://www.ideaconnection.com/right-brain-workouts/00193-cross-pollination-how-and-why-it-works.html

Pasini, R. (2016, January 26). The Compliment Sandwich: How To Give Constructive Criticism Without Hurting People's Feelings. Retrieved January, 2017, from http://bewellplace.com/the-compliment-sandwich-how-to-give-constructive-criticism-without-hurting-peoples-feelings/

■ Meetings

Millennials hate meetings! They're (one of) the most overused business activities. One of the quickest ways to disengage anyone is to put them in a meeting that's of zero value to them. If they don't need to be there, get them out! Meetings should be used for one of three reasons:

» To make money

» To make decisions

» To make both

Sitting there and chatting with no clear agenda or outcome is a complete waste of time. If a meeting is just there to shove information down someone's throat for an hour, stop. No one wants to see management beat their chest and tell everyone what needs to change. All that information can be squeezed into one email (or video) for everyone to read or watch on their own time. If you're going to have a meeting with millennials, make sure that everyone's voice will get heard. Millennials are all about meetings if they're purpose driven and collaboration based.

Management must start using better discretion when planning and organizing meetings. I've sat in too many hour-long meetings that could have easily been cut down to 20 minutes. Why waste all that time? Let's break it down:

If you have a one-hour meeting and there are 40 employees in the room, that's 40 man hours of productivity. That's one person's total output for one week that was thrown out the window for a meeting. You better make sure that the one-hour meeting those 40 people are sitting through is well worth the time. One week of productivity is no joke!

Bad meetings make disengagement go viral. If it can be put in an email or training video, do that. If it's important that everyone have input on the conversation, that's great. Send out an email with what will be covered for the meeting, schedule a time, cover it concisely, make decisions, then set time aside after the fact to implement those action items.

There are some organizations that have Monday and Friday meetings "just because," and that's fine. I get that it's part of how things work for some companies. If it's a complete necessity to have those gatherings, make sure management adds some fun and engagement in the meeting. Not everything within the meeting has to be stiff. Have some fun with it. The way your meetings run is a physical representation of your company culture.

Meetings can be:

» A place to share concerns (culture of transparency).

» A place to laugh about success and horror stories from the week (culture of fun / family / relaxing).

» A place to share ideas (culture of innovation).

» A place to share best practices (culture of peak performance).

» A place to have games and competitions for prizes (culture of competitive spirit).

Meetings are a leverage point that can be used effectively. But most often, they're a waste of time, money and energy.

Jeff Bezos (CEO of Amazon) has the two-pizza rule for meetings. This rule states that, <u>if you can't feed the whole meeting with two pizzas, there are too many people at the table</u> (somewhere around eight people) (1). I agree with this if the purpose of the meeting is to make direct decisions. However, if the sales team of 100 people needs to meet, then get everyone in the same room, keep them engaged, and have a good time with it. Bezos claims that over-communication results in a drop of productivity. If someone doesn't need to be in the meeting, get them out!

How companies use meetings says a lot about the management of an organization. The way meetings are leveraged is either driving the company forward or holding it back. Meetings are the company's platform for awareness on both a corporate and individual level.

Engaging meetings typically challenge millennials in the best way possible. They break down generational gaps by getting an honest look at where the company is at and where it's going. Candid discussions during meetings will help millennials get a grasp on the next steps they need to take. Used properly, meetings can create unprecedented momentum, but if used improperly, meetings can be the beginning of the end.

Jeff Bezos' two-pizza rule for building productive teams. (2016, November 22). Retrieved January, 2017, from http://www.bizjournals.com/bizjournals/how-to/human-resources/2016/11/jeff-bezos-two-pizza-rule-for-building-productive.html

■ Professional Courtesy

Many baby boomers feel that millennials have no professional courtesy. We walk a fine line between projecting confidence and arrogance (1). We walk a fine line between asking questions and being nosy. Every day we fight the battle between engaging with our peers online and limiting our personal screen time (1). There are many millennials who don't consider professionalism as part of their work life. The people in this generation who are aware of professional courtesy will thrive within multi-generational interactions.

What we do in business is very important. But, *how* we do it is what we'll be remembered by. If corporations want to ensure multi-generational engagement and transparency, then it's imperative that millennials both give and receive professional courtesy.

There's nothing worse than seeing a well-accomplished individual be discourteous to another. It makes us look at that person differently. Situations like this usually arise because (sometimes) successful people think they're better than others.

Over the years, I've befriended a gentleman named Brad Pierce, the president of Restaurant Equipment World. Brad's an extremely successful entrepreneur who flies his plane across the country to attend his meetings. I've taken some good pointers from him over the years, and this was one of them.

Brad told me that he's the poor guy in his group of friends. (I told him that means he's hanging out with the right people)! The point is, Brad constantly surrounds himself with other successful entrepreneurs. He has told me that he's always looking for patterns his friends have that he can implement in his own life. He's shared with me that the <u>number one commonality amongst his successful friends is courtesy</u>.

When you're dealing with a waitress, stewardess, or even someone at the front desk of a hotel, it's important to treat those people with respect and honor. How you treat someone that's serving you is indicative of how you would treat any other person you have a relationship with. Waiters and hotel staff are always getting emotionally bullied by guests, so be the light. Be the customer that they're excited to see walk through the door. Be the guy that's going to make their job exciting and not dreadful. This leads into a concept I spoke about during my TEDx Talk, bucket filling versus bucket dipping.

Our bucket of water is a metaphor for our self-confidence. By handing out compliments, and words of encouragement, we're filling that person's bucket and also our own. By making fun of people, and bringing them down, we're dipping from their bucket as well as our own.

It's a simple concept when you think about it. In any interaction, we're either adding to someone's life or taking away from it. The quality of our personal lives is directly correlated to how many buckets we either fill or empty. I think it's obvious which is the better choice.

When we're a jerk to others, the people who have to work for you will only do what they're told. They may not like you, but they'll most likely get the job done. However, if you're the light in the room, the people who <u>have to</u>

work for you will <u>want to</u> work for you. They'll want to help you succeed. They'll want to make your life easier, and they'll want to <u>go the extra mile</u> to make sure your needs are met. The bottom line is that successful people know how to get others to go that extra mile, and it makes a huge difference. If you want others to go the extra mile, it starts with professional courtesy.

This principle goes across all areas of our lives. When we're the source of empowerment, everyone steps up to the plate. Everyone's bucket is getting filled and the tide is rising. Ever heard the quote, "A rising tide raises all boats?" If we make sure everyone's boats are just a little bit higher, people will go out of their way to make our lives that much easier.

There's a fundamental difference between <u>having</u> to go to work tomorrow and <u>wanting</u> to go to work tomorrow. Having professional courtesy could be the little thing that makes a difference in someone's day.

Brad ensured me that this advice would not be a disservice to me. So far, he's right. I've watched many millennials succeed because of their professional courtesy, and others perish because of their lack of awareness. Enlightening people has given me opportunities way beyond my reach. If you're the type of person people want to surround themselves with, you'll find a way to create the relationships to catalyze your success. So, put a smile on. You never know who's watching.

Silverthorn, M. (2015, January 30). 20 Professionalism Tips for Millennials. Retrieved January, 2017, from https://www.linkedin.com/pulse/20-professionalism-tips-millennials-michelle-silverthorn

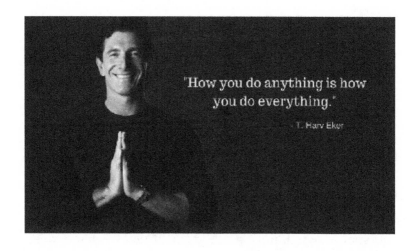

"How you do anything is how you do everything."

- T. Harv Eker

■ Transparency

Openness. Honesty. Sincerity. In a world that has become increasingly sensationalistic, these are qualities that are valued now more than ever. Our public sector and healthcare system hold information back from us to "protect us." I call it bullshit. They call it "public safety." It doesn't matter what you call it; just know that corporate ambiguity will be short lived.

As millennials gain influence and power, transparency will not be asked for; it will be demanded. If people choose to not be transparent and honest, then they will lose to people who are. We would rather hear the cold hard truth than some bullshit political rhetoric about how you "did everything you could." Those people and businesses will soon be on their way out, and sincere heroes will be on their way in.

We're seeing authenticity from people across the world on social media voicing their opinions, and hoping that someone hears them. "Me! Me! Me! Pick *me*! Listen to *me*! Hear *me* out!" People with a voice have platforms to share their insights, and they should use those platforms to express themselves with transparency. Straightforwardness has become a less common characteristic in a world full of smoke and mirrors.

As corporations start employing more millennials, they need to realize that the flow of information within the company needs to flow in both directions, from top to bottom and back up again. If you want to retain millennials, then you must be sure that you give them an opportunity to express themselves openly and honestly. Give them a platform to share their ideas instead of condemning them to the confines of "what was." Millennials can help you stop talking about "what was," and start talking about "what is" and "what's going to be." Those are much more important topics of conversation.

It's okay to give millennials your honest feedback, just as they gave you theirs. But, there are many supervisors who look at insight from younger professionals as threatening. I've too often heard of people being open about their opinions. Then suddenly, Monday morning, they're fired.

Transparency means sharing truths about the company, providing feedback on performance, and encouraging communication (1). A difference in opinions doesn't show a lack of integrity. It takes courage to stand up in front of your superiors and be 100% honest. Don't knock it; encourage it.

At the end of the day we're all just humans, sitting in a room and making decisions. Thinking that your decisions can't be positively affected by a millennial's perspective is shortsighted. They have insight that you don't have and vice versa. The book *Think and Grow Rich* talks about the concept that two minds together inevitably create a third mind much more powerful than the sum of both. This mastermind principle can only be leveraged in an atmosphere of transparency. It must be ingrained in not only our culture, but also in our personal philosophy if we are to grow and thrive in this new age.

The Value of Transparency to Millennial Employees | ORC Intl. (2015, December 02). Retrieved January, 2017, from https://orcinternational.com/employee-

_engagement/the-val-ue-of-transparency-to-millennial-
employees/_

What We Expect

■ Identity Training

Training is by far my favorite topic. It's truly the Achilles' heel of 21st century business. Acquiring, training, and retaining talent is the name of the game.

Quality training can be one of the top acquisition and retention strategies if it's used effectively. Training can help millennials experience the profound growth that they've always desired.

Training can be thought of under two lights. Role training and identity training.

Role training teaches someone how to be <u>the best employee possible</u>.

Identity training teaches someone how to become <u>the best version of themselves</u>.

Most companies completely miss the boat on identity training. They write it off as "not their responsibility" or "secondary to role training." In the 21st century, that assumption could be the beginning of the end; especially if you plan on retaining millennials.

Let's play a quick game of "this or that":

» Employee centric companies or customer centric companies?

» Hard skills (technical training) or soft skills (leadership, creativity, innovation, etc.)?

One could easily make an argument for both sides of each question. In my opinion, there is *nothing* more important than invigorating your employees to become the best version of themselves. Many of the soft skills in business are blown over by management. <u>The people who have the soft skills (management) don't need it, and the people that need it (regular employees) don't have it</u>. There is an invisible ROI in business – and quite often management has a hard time rationalizing investments into activities that don't show a direct correlation to increased profit. Relationship building. Company culture. Personal Development. Team interconnectedness. Aspects of business like these have an invisible ROI – they're valuable to people, not balance sheets.

Strong people turn into strong employees, which create strong companies. <u>However, strong companies start with strong people. And, strong people need to be trained how to wake up every day and push to become the best version of themselves</u>. This applies to everyone; not just millennials.

During my time with Tony Robbins, I worked with companies in dozens of different industries. I was able to get insight into the way training was done, and the way training should have been done. Every company teaches people how to be a good employee, but quite frankly, most don't even do that well. Very few companies teach people how to become the best version of themselves. Training is typically the first line item cut within a corporate budget. According to a VC (venture capitalist) I've spoken with, most venture-backed companies have $0 allocated toward training. Many venture capitalists feel that their startups don't have the time for non-technical training. The big companies think their training is 'sufficient,' and the small companies write it off as fluff.

Imagine if you handed a potential millennial employee an offer and told them this: "Here's the deal.

Not only am I going to pay you $XX,XXX and give you these benefits, but I'm going to train you to wake up every day and be the person you've always known you could become. I'm going to teach you how to do more, be more, have more, laugh more, and create more. And, I can promise you with every ounce of certainty in my body that you will go through this employment experience and grow as an individual just as much as an employee. It's my obligation to make sure you become the best version of yourself. You in?"

Is there any employee on the planet that wouldn't buy into that vision? Millennials want to learn the soft skills necessary for them to thrive in any environment. Often, we forget that <u>who we are</u> and <u>what we do</u> for work are two completely different stories. We tend to think that our LinkedIn profile and resume define us. But, who would you be if you stripped away all of your professional accomplishments and accolades? That's what identity training and soft skill training is all about.

Millennial employees are consistently searching for ways to become the best version of themselves. To tap into our full personal potential, there are a few tricks of the trade. Peak performance is about growing to new heights, but the most efficient way to raise the bar is to increase our average performance.

It seems counterintuitive, but have you ever seen someone that's incredible at what they do? Of course, you have. What's the first thing you typically say? It's usually something along the lines of, "Wow, they make it look easy."

These professionals make it look easy because they've steadily increased their average. Their average performance tends to look like an all-star performance. And when they're really at their peak, that special person comes out. They're so in the zone, and in tune with their most successful identity that they become unstoppable. They are congruent, and energetically aligned with the highest version of themselves. The recorded moments of these experiences can be seen across sports, entertainment, business, and even politics. The people who shine in these moments are the ones who have pushed to discover themselves at the deepest level, and steadily increase their average performance.

We all have a success identity, and the purpose of identity training is to teach us how to find that version of ourselves and call upon it at any time.

Gradually increasing our average performance is all about habits and patterns. Our success identity is based around success rituals. We are what we repeatedly do, so some of identity training involves pattern recognition and pattern disruption. Becoming self-aware of our habits, both the ones that drive us forward and the ones that hold us back, will propel us down the path toward peak performance. The best version of ourselves is a certain pattern.

As T. Harv Eker said, how we do anything is how we do everything. If we're stressed out at work, we could also be stressed out in our personal life. If our living area is disorganized, our work area most likely looks the same. This means that a problem within the workplace could be manifested from a bad relationship, health, lack of sleep, or any number of other personal issues.

Bosses tend to assume that a problem within the workplace has caused the employee to disengage, but that couldn't be further from the truth. As a manager, it's your responsibility to uncover the problem, which means being self-aware enough to realize that problems are typically multifaceted. Because of that, managers must be willing to dive deep into difficulties of their employees, and take a more holistic approach to problem solving.

It's important that managers become mindful of the individual strengths of each team member. Management can teach someone to be an awesome person, but if they're in the wrong seat at the table, management is wasting their energy. An employee's scope of work should have the five things that the person does best, not the description that's found online.

It's not our job to be good at everything the company does. It's our job to be good at a few things. If our job entails those few things, management is making it that much easier for us to become the best versions of ourselves every day.

It's important to create a training program that bridges the gap between corporate growth and employee growth. Being an incredible person is just as important as being an incredible employee. Incredible people become incredible employees, incredible employees create incredible companies, and incredible companies change the world.

Role Training

Now that we've discussed how employees can become the best version of themselves, we must teach them the skills necessary to succeed within their scope of work. Millennials are looking for management to show them the relevancy of specific training to the overall picture. Creating a digital platform will allow millennials to follow a training process step by step and track their progress.

The key to quality training is to do a little bit daily. Millennials like short, three to five minute videos with an activity at the end of each. Too many training programs have one-hour videos that aren't concise in their delivery. I remember the training program I did for an internship at Northwestern Mutual back in the day. Incredible company, awesome training, but it was poorly executed.

The first week of the job was all training, 9 a.m. to 5 p.m. Monday – Friday. 40 hours. Then we're off to the races.

Conceptually it was good, but in application it was terrible. We were inundated with information in four-hour stints, twice a day. At the end of that week we were expected to apply of all that information. Here's the problem: no one remembered the information when they needed it.

Don't get it twisted – I have nothing against Northwestern. They're an incredible company. Most companies make the whole first week training, then throw their employees out to the sharks. Many employees finish their second week of work feeling incompetent because they failed (miserably,) and didn't use any of the training they were provided. This does more harm than good.

Training works best when an employee is immersed at the beginning of the experience, and then given new content on a weekly basis. This allows supervisors to gradually create new instruction as problems arise. This also allows management to give millennials feedback as they progress through the training process. With this type of feedback loop, millennials have the opportunity to give management insight as to how the companies training can grow over time.

Are you having a communication problem within the office? Create a couple of three to five minute videos to work out the issues. Now, new employees can be on the same page and reference the training when necessary. This means managers don't have to waste time solving the same problem all over again.

Thirty minutes of training a day should be good, give or take. Consistently creating new training allows organizations to adapt to the inevitable obstacles faced in business. Quality training is one of the best ways to gradually improve any company over time.

The training your company implements is part of the culture, and company culture is implemented from the top down, but innovated from the bottom up. Company culture must be innovated from the bottom up because the employees on the front lines can see change before anyone else. It's important to empathize with the team and ask them what they're struggling with. If management is self-aware, structuring training around problems will solve the new operational inefficiencies that periodically arise.

When looking to create quality training, <u>the key is to discover the specific outcome you're looking for and then reverse engineer the solution</u>. The goal is to create a step by step system for peak performance. I'll give you the perfect example.

Many of the people I train are in the sales industry. It's by far the most common profession in America today. Let's take a realtor for instance. There are (at least) two million realtors out there, and a majority make below a living wage (under 3 houses per year) (1). Note that many of them work part-time.

"Bob Smith" is a realtor struggling with sales. Bob comes up to me and says, "Jesse, I really need help selling more houses. I'm only selling one house per year. I'm not sure what I'm doing wrong. What should I do?"

I'll respond with a simple question like, "What's your profession again?" They'll look at me like I'm a little crazy. "Well, I'm a realtor. But you knew that already."

Of course, I do, I'm just starting off with the basics. "So, tell me, Bob, what is the primary function of a realtor?" This is a trap question; they just don't realize it.

"Jesse, come on, man, I'm a realtor. I'm in the business of selling houses."

I'll stare at them, hoping that they realize the vital mistake they just made. Typically, they don't realize what they said has a huge fundamental flaw in it.

"Look, you're struggling in your business because you're not applying the sales process. In its simplest form, the sales process looks like this: Get the lead. Qualify the lead into a prospect. Introduce yourself. Build rapport. Get the client to commit with an upfront contract. Uncover the need / pain. Satisfy the need pain. Overcome objections.

Close the deal." Sometimes the order of the process gets moved around, but that's the gist of it.

Someone like Bob will typically roll their eyes at me, thinking something like, 'Wow, he really thinks I don't understand sales.' No, it has nothing to do with that. It has to do with the fact that we're skipping steps. We're skipping steps because many training programs show the end result (selling a house) without walking employees through the process step by step.

I'll say something like this. "Listen, Bob, you say you're in the business of selling houses, but you can't sell a house until you generate a lead and build a relationship." He'll look at me with a blank stare. "Bob, you're not in the business of selling houses, you're in the business of generating leads and building relationships. Now, tell me, Bob, what's your lead generation strategy, and how do you go about building rapport with people?"

You might as well have brought in a bunch of aliens to speak with Bob. His head was in outer space.

He's been thinking this whole time he's in the business of selling houses, when he's really in the business of generating leads and building relationships. It's a paradigm shift in thinking for someone who is in the sales industry.

Here's the fundamental problem. The larger real estate brokerages tend to focus on teaching agents how to sell a house, but who cares? Knowing how to sell a house is useless if agents don't know how to generate leads.

» Step One: Generate leads

» Step Two: Build relationships

» Final Step: Sell house

There are many steps that go in between building relationships and selling. But, who cares if you know how to sell, <u>if you can't generate quality leads in the first place</u>?

What I'm trying to say is this: the biggest mistake professionals make in the business world is that they try to take step 10 (or step 100) before they take step 1. Step one is the only thing you need to focus on when you're getting started. Step one is the starting point of infinite momentum. But, most importantly, step one leads to step two! Business is about putting one foot in front of the other, not trying to skip your way to the sale. Bob's lack of sales can be attributed to a broken training process. He was extremely competent; he just wasn't properly trained on how to generate leads and build relationships. These are the first steps that new sales people must master.

Most people get extremely intimidated by step 100. They'll say something like, "Damn, it's going to take a lot of work to accomplish that goal." Most notably, they'll say this before they even take the first step.

This can all be avoided with one easy solution: quality training. Focus on training people how to take the first step. Simplify it to the point where a child could do it. Follow up with them in person, and make sure they've mastered step one during the first week. Then move on to step two and so on. Millennials are looking for training to be a coaching process; one where there's a conversation and feedback loop to maximize growth. Stop trying to teach your employees the last step before they take the first. They get mentally caught up in the end game and write off the basics as unnecessary. Therefore, it's important to reverse engineer the outcomes the business needs in a training program. The methodical, step by step approach will help an employee thrive in the long run. Too many companies are just focused on getting a new hire the first sale as quickly as possible. Employers take a net loss on a new hire until that person starts generating revenue. There's nothing wrong with sales, but if employers are looking for longevity in their employees, following a proven training process is the key to success.

If the company you work at is not constantly developing and improving its training, they're losing out to the organization who is. Quality training will push employees to grow beyond what they think they're capable of. They'll constantly be trying new things and, most likely, failing. If they're experiencing failure, then they're on the right track. It means they're trying something different. Millennials aren't afraid of failing if there's an infrastructure to support their attempts. Training can provide a tangible base for employees to progress within their role. Valuable training creates constant and never ending improvement within the organization. It's one of those things that will have positive, long term effects that customers may never see.

How many homes per year does the "average" real estate agent sell? (2015, April 08). Retrieved January, 2017, from http://www.zillow.com/advice-thread/How-many-homes-per-year-does-the-average-real-estate-agent-sell/582119/

I NEVER LOSE
I EITHER WIN
OR LEARN

- Nelson Mandela

▪ Growth

The opposite of growth is decay, and, if you're not moving forward in life, you're getting left behind. Millennials have a growth mindset, and for longevity purposes, companies would benefit from adopting this ideology. The millennial mindset accounts for up to 50 percent of a brands performance (1). This 'new age perspective' is not confined to an age range, which means companies targeting the millennial mindset will deal with consumers from many different backgrounds and demographics. Targeting an ideology and targeting an age group are two separate battles. The growth mindset can help companies both employ and sell to people with this type of perspective.

Successful people are comfortable with being uncomfortable because they know that growth happens at the edge of their comfort zone. In the most general sense, I look at growth in terms of personally, professionally, mentally, physically, spiritually, and emotionally. There are different strokes for different folks. Everyone looks at growth a little differently. But the bottom line is, if you're not changing, you're not growing.

Let's take the example of the saying, "An overnight success is 10 years in the making." If there are 365 days in a year, in 10 years, there are (about) 3,650 days.

If you improve 1% every day, physically, mentally, spiritually, emotionally, professionally or personally in any way possible, you're on the right track. No matter how you define growth, it's important to ideologically push the limits on a consistent basis. If you improve your life by 1% every day for 3,650 days, what's going to happen? You'll eventually turn into an "overnight success."

I spoke about this concept in my TEDx Talk. I referred to it as the aggregation of marginal gains. This concept is also commonly referred to as the compound effect, or the snowball effect.

If you're standing on a mountain and throw a snowball at a tree, the snowball breaks into a million pieces. If instead of a snowball you have an avalanche moving down that mountain, it's going to take out every tree in its path.

For all intents and purposes, let's call this avalanche 3,650% more powerful than the snowball. In life, you need to be able to knock down any trees that get in your way. If you crumble when life puts trees in your way, you'll never find true success. Is this starting to make sense?

The whole goal is to just push ourselves a little further each day. All the magic in life happens when we push a little beyond what we were previously capable of. Comfort can be dangerous, so those who face it (yet desire growth) must always make the choice to push through. In life, you can't forget that you're either moving forward or getting left behind. Millennials are looking to get stronger, push farther, and grow faster. Companies will benefit if they support that ideology with resources.

When I first started working for Tony, a guy walked up to me after one of my workshops and said, "I'm not getting better or worse. I'm just staying the same. That's the way I want it."

I said, "Listen, if that's where you want to be in life, I won't try to convince you otherwise." He had a grin of satisfaction.

I waited a few seconds and then said, "You gotta realize, our economy, our society and life in general grows by 3% per year. That's just inflation. So, if you're staying the same and everything else in the world is increasing by 3%, then you're actually falling behind." The inflationary perspective tends to throw people off.

Then, you always get the smart ass who states, "Well, what if I'm improving by exactly 3% per year?"

My thought process behind that line of thinking is, "Screw that!" If you want to be average, then be content with a 3% increase from last year. I'll be working toward 365% growth, while helping others do the same. It's a great mentality for any individual or organization. There are many golden nuggets within this book to help you create your own avalanche. It's up to you to define how you'd like to grow on a consistent basis.

These percentages are all ideological representations of growth. Growth is a mindset. If you want to grow, become mindful of where you're at and where you need to go. The formula is quite simple:

Awareness + Energy = Momentum

» Awareness is about understanding what's going on (both beyond and within). Most people on this planet are asleep; they just happen to have their eyes open. We need to be mentally, physically, spiritually and emotionally conscious of where we're at in relation to our surroundings. Awareness is all about the moment, and having a complete understanding of who we are, what we want, where we are going, when we're going to make our next move, and why we're making it. Using all that information, we decide <u>how</u> we're going to get there. When we're aware, we're able to decide which beliefs will drive us forward, and which ones will hold us back. Becoming aware is an empowering action, and one that will allow us to infinitely grow over time. Any mistake we've made in our past has probably resulted from a slight lack of awareness. Different situations require different actions, and awareness helps people make beneficial decisions on a consistent basis. Think about awareness as your snowball.

» Energy is life. Everything we hear, see, taste, touch and smell is energy. Energy is not only limited to our perceptions, but encompasses the entire universe. <u>The electrons in every particle everywhere are moving</u> **(2).** <u>If every electron retains energy, then energy is the common denominator of all existence</u>. The law of conservation of energy states, "energy can neither be created nor destroyed; rather, it transforms from one form to another." All the energy in the world already exists; all we have to do is figure out how to move it in the direction we want it to go. To move energy, we must understand how to control our own energy. <u>One of the most incredible skills a person can acquire is the ability to control energy</u>. When we look at *emotion* on a scale of *positive to negative*, and energy on a scale from *low to high*, we get this graph.

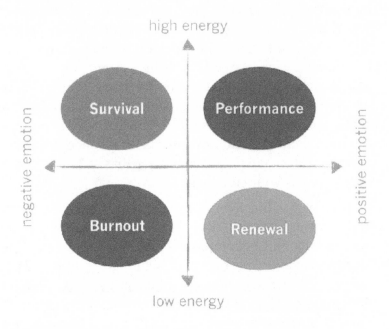

high energy

Survival | Performance

negative emotion | positive emotion

Burnout | Renewal

low energy

Awareness is the ability to recognize where we sit on this chart at any point in time. If we are aware in the present moment and use positive emotions, we can begin (or continue to) create our avalanche. All growth in this world takes place with positive high energy. Positive low energy helps us get ready for more high energy. You may start to look at everything start thinking about things in terms of the transfer of energy. Energy is what can turn any snowball into an avalanche.

» Momentum is probably the most addicting drug on the planet. Momentum is why the rich get richer, the poor get poorer, and the mediocre stay mediocre. That's Newton's First Law of Motion: an object in motion tends to stay in motion. Momentum is an avalanche, an unstoppable force that refuses to slow down. Momentum will allow us to mow down any tree in our way. With enough momentum, we can accomplish anything.

It's all about <u>energy awareness</u>. The conscious use of energy, and the understanding how to manage and control it, will allow us to develop the momentum needed to cultivate our ideal outcomes. If we want to grow, this is the starting point. Understanding ourselves, our surroundings, and the energy we must exert to get to our next level. Your journey is unique to you. And the way to create a great journey is to just start putting one foot in front of the other. The first step is the most painful, but the one that leads to all the pleasure you've ever desired. In today's age, there are so many touch points and resources available to help us create momentum.

Millennials are the first generation to truly leverage technology for growth. An article quoting Ian Bogost, a professor at Georgia Tech, talks about the many benefits technology can have on development. He mentions enhanced learning and retention, improved concentration and multi-tasking ability, better cooperation and teamwork, and growing confidence and self-esteem (3). If properly monitored, technology can undoubtedly help society become more resourceful over time.

There is also a group of people out there who believe that humans are evolving into a new species called 'homo-sentient'. They argue that we are emerging as a species beyond the homo-sapiens, which means "wiseman", and becoming homo-sentients, meaning *'aware or conscious man'* (4). They argue that this new state of being has bridged the gap between mind, body, and spirit. Although I do think that our species has evolved into a more aware version of ourselves, I don't believe that we are actually a different species; just simply a more evolved version of the species we've always been. I don't foresee a future in which homo-sapiens can't reproduce with the "more evolved" homo-sentients. Something like that happens over thousands of years of evolution.

Similar to the "homo-sentient" ideology, Juan Enriquez references the term "homo-evolutis" to describe a more advanced species in his TEDx Talk, *The Next Species of Human* (5). He defines this species as "hominids that take direct and deliberate control over the evolution of their species... and others." There's no doubt that we're becoming a more evolved, aware, and resourceful species. However, I'm cautious about classifying us as a new species, separate from the one we've always been. It'll be interesting to see how the human race grows and evolves over the next century. It's going to be one hell of a ride!

Growth can be an emotional rollercoaster, one that millennials are excited to go on. Our individual evolution and progression occurs every moment, and it's a byproduct of everything that's ever been, and the momentum we've created for ourselves. Every day is full of highs and lows, U-turns and nose dives. Hopefully, as you continue to go down your path of growth, you'll start to realize that your destination is you journey. It's your never-ending mountain. The steeper the climb, the better the view. Just make sure you don't let any trees get in your way.

How to Identify New Growth Potential with the Millennial Mindset®. (n.d.). Retrieved January, 2017, from http://www.millennialmarketing.com/2016/04/how-to-identify-new-growth-potential-with-the-millennial-mindset/

Always in Motion. (n.d.). Retrieved January, 2017, from
http://www.chem4kids.com/files/atom_orbital.html

Steinberg, S. (2016, June 27). 5 Reasons That Technology Is Good for Kids. Retrieved January, 2017, from http://parade.com/485609/scott_steinberg/5-reasons-that-technology-is-good-for-kids/

HOMO-SENTIENTS: Coming Out of the 3-Dimensional Box. (2011, February 20). Retrieved January, 2017, from http://vividlife.me/ultimate/12024/homo-sentients-coming-outof-the-3-dimensional-box/

Enriquez, J. (2009, February). The next species of human. Retrieved January, 2017, from https://www.ted.com/talks/juan_enriquez_shares_min dboggling_new_science#t-1094243

P.S. – If you don't like the formula (<u>Awareness + Energy</u> = <u>Momentum</u>) that's perfectly fine! Maybe you should ask yourself this question:

What is my personal formula for success or happiness?

■ Innovation

Millennials want to create a company's products with them. They want to hold your hand and be a part of the process every step of the way. This goes for both employees and customers. By changing innovation to a co-creation process, companies can leverage the millennial's feedback and iterate their offerings quicker than ever before.

It's my belief that many companies shy away from a co-creation process because they fear constructive criticism. We live in an age where bad reviews on Yelp or Amazon can have a significant impact on sales. If a company encourages constructive criticism, the reviews could negatively impact other consumer's perceptions about the product.

Asking for constructive criticism takes courage, but millennials respect that. If you ask them their opinion, they'll give it to you. Non-sugar coated, quality feedback. If you implement their innovations, you'll start to evangelize your most vocal consumers.

In today's age, the lifecycle of products has dramatically shortened. Large companies are putting out multiple new products every single year. Innovation is what the growth of their business is really based upon. Most companies are partially in the research business; they just don't always listen to the data.

Products are implemented from the top down, but they're innovated from the bottom up.

Innovation should always be a bottom-up process. To properly understand what to innovate, companies need to take a grassroots approach with both customers and employees. The people on the front lines of the workforce understand the customer's psychology, and how the company can better support them. Innovation comes in many forms including:

» Process

» Culture

» Product / service

» Training

» Customer service

» Sales

» Support structure

Innovation is a cornerstone of 21st century companies, but many of them don't take the right approach to this activity. Organizations start providing products and services, but those offerings can only be improved through quality feedback.

Innovation can come from any employee, any customer, or any partnership. A Deloitte study said that 78% of millennials are influenced by how innovative a company is when deciding if they wanted to work there (1). Millennials want to work for companies that foster innovation. That's great news because there's always a way to improve something within any organization. Executives can't be afraid to confront the brutal facts of business, and fact number one is that your company is not perfect, and it never will be. Every business has a system that helped them yesterday, but may hurt them today. What got the company to where it is, isn't necessarily what will get them to where they're going (based on the book title by Marshall Goldsmith: *What Got You Here Won't Get You There*). If organizations create a culture of innovation, the company will be sure to constantly thrive and grow.

Tony Robbins taught me that there are two things that every great company has: quality marketing and innovation. Innovation comes from within someone. That organization must have an innate desire to improve, or innovation will just fizzle out. If your organization is always creating new offerings and properly marketing them to your customers, you'll always appeal to those with a growth mindset. Millennials love change, and change should be your businesses best friend. It's when you start to get comfortable with what you have, that everything can fall apart.

Millennial Survey 2014 | Deloitte | Social impact, Innovation. (2016, January 22). Retrieved January, 2017, from http://www2.deloitte.com/al/en/pages/about-deloitte/articles/2014-millennial-survey-positive-impact.html

■ Communication

If we want to influence a millennial, we must understand what already influences them. Honesty. Feedback. Growth. Wittiness. Passion. Optimism. Mobile. New techniques. These are all things that millennials look for when communicating with others.

Communication is the catalyst to human collaboration. Without proper communication skills, businesses and people will falter. Strong communication is the basis for all relationships, whether they are physical or digital.

Communication is based upon the sharing of knowledge and information. In the good ole' days, you were encouraged to keep knowledge close to your chest. If your competitor finds it out, they could copy you!

Today, if your competitor wants to copy you, they will. Keeping trade secrets is important, and I encourage you to do so, but we must realize that in the 21st century, the sharing of knowledge opens the flood gates of opportunity. Elon Musk released all the Tesla patents to the public to help spur innovation in his industry (1). This is a great example of leaders stepping up the plate to help others foster innovation and creativity.

I have self-proclaimed myself as a knowledge socialist (not to be confused with the political philosophy). I enjoy spreading knowledge. It's all about equal opportunity baby! The more informed people are; the better decisions they make. The Internet has allowed us to share knowledge like never before.

In today's world, when new products are put out, communication ramps up. There are new wikis, blogs, reviews and posts online. We are entering a world where every business will need some form of content strategy. Videos, podcasts, blogs, articles, and contributing posts on other sites help companies reach new target demographics. Content marketing helps drive search results and optimization for products and services.

The increase of digital communication has shortened product lifecycles because the information now travels quicker. Products get used and reviewed instantly, and now the market is waiting for the next great thing – this is both good and bad.

When communicating, it's imperative that you speak from a place of honesty and truth no matter what your level of authority is (2). It's important to maintain good eye contact and open body language. Actively listening can help engage the person you're speaking with and progress the conversation forward. Some of you may be thinking of these things as obvious, but the art of communication has suffered defeat from the age of technology. Millennials tend not to value face-to-face communication as highly as their elders. We have used technology as a communication crutch and (some of us) have rendered face-to-face interactions as useless. Millennials who leverage face-to-face interactions are miles ahead of their peers.

Older generations have now started using emoji's, hashtags and millennial lingo to assimilate to this generation. Although I can appreciate the attempt to build rapport, just because someone speaks and writes like a millennial doesn't mean they think like one. If you want to empathize with us, adopt (or at least recognize) our ideology. It's the only way *The Millennial Merger* will positively impact an organization.

One of the toughest things an elder can do is make an age joke. When I was speaking for Tony, I would get responses like, "You're only 23/24. What do you know about beliefs and patterns?" Or "Before you were born, there was a time when I was doing."

When speaking with elders, I typically hear them talk only about the past. I try to have as many conversations as possible about today and tomorrow – I'm always looking to move forward. The only time yesterday is impactful is if there are key distinctions I can use to better my life moving forward. Communicating on the same wavelength is crucial if we're going to successfully merge ideologies moving forward.

Communication is how we learn and grow both personally and professionally. Modern face to face communication has a lot to do with the beliefs of the individuals communicating.

» If you believe that there's something more important on your phone than what that person has to say, that will get translated.

» If you believe that what you have to say is more important than what they're talking about, that will get translated.

» If you believe that the person you're speaking with is interesting, and you can learn something by talking with them, that will get translated as well.

Humans can intuitively understand belief systems. If your beliefs align with your actions, then your communication will come off as congruent.

Congruency is harmony. When you are congruent, your thoughts, emotions, words, actions and physiology are all moving in the same direction. Congruency is influence.

We've all spoken to someone whose thoughts are going forward, their emotions are moving backward, their words are all over the place, and mentally, they're a mess. Those people don't propel us into action because they aren't aligned.

So, when you're communicating with a millennial, come from a place of passion and excitement. Become optimistic, but don't be afraid to be witty and truthful. Give them constructive criticism and ask for it in return. If you communicate with a sense of honesty and transparency, then building rapport with a millennial will be easier than ever.

The most important communication concept covered here is congruency. Congruency expresses drive, will, conviction and determination when communicating with others. It shows people that you're confident in who you are, where you're going, and how you're going to get there. Congruency will turn you into an influencer, and in the 21st century, influencers always win.

Musk, E. (2014, August 19). All Our Patent Are Belong To You. Retrieved January, 2017, from https://www.tesla.com/blog/all-our-patent-are-belong-you

Attracting and Retaining Millennials in the Global Workplace. (2016, June 24). Retrieved January, 2017, from http://www.aperianglobal.com/attracting-retaining-millennials-global-workplace/

■ Touch – Internet – Phone – (T.I.P)

Knowing how to TIP, and teaching others how to TIP, is one of the most crucial communication concepts in modern times. TIP stands for:

» **Touch** – face to face (physical interactions)

» **Internet** – email / social media / search

» **Phone** – talk / text / video chat

TIP represents the many different types of communication we use daily. Many employers completely blow over these concepts during the training process. Millennials tend to have the Internet down pat, but need help when it comes to phone and in-person communication.

When people communicate with each other, their emotions change in a moment's notice. New conversations lead to new thoughts, questions, answers, decisions, and actions. These conversations can be with ourselves, or another person – and these conversations are what solidify, or change, our beliefs. Here's a visual representation of how communication is supposed to look. Realistically speaking though, emotions, thoughts, and questions periodically arise out of order because; shit happens.

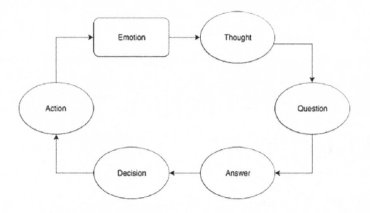

Communication is the foundation of humanity, and no matter how advanced technology gets, this will always remain true. Based on the previous chart, our future is determined by:

» The emotions we feel.

» The thoughts we think.

» The questions we ask, and the answers they create.

» The decisions we make.

» The actions we take.

» Our ability to reevaluate.

Our ability to change the meaning of circumstances throughout our lives will determine how we deal with pain, and how we use it to drive us forward. If we have the power to change the meaning of a situation, we have the power to change our lives.

The result of all that we truly desire in life are certain feelings and emotions. The way we communicate with each other has a dramatic impact on our emotional states. Here's a brief outline on how to T.I.P in the 21st century.

Touch

Some millennials have lost the ability to properly engage in a face-to-face situation. I would bet that this problem will only get worse as the generations continue. I refuse to let the millennials be the generation that let the art of face-to-face communication die. Technology has made in person interactions obsolete for millennials who prefer written communication (1). Virtual businesses run all over the world, and that's great, but the art of the human interaction needs to be upheld. It's important that employees know how to properly engage in a face to face conversation.

Are you doing things like:

» Maintaining eye contact – this one is probably the biggest

» Point your feet toward the person you're engaging with

» Shoulders back, deep breathing, neck up

» Smiling

» Asking Questions

» Actively Listening

» Engaging hands

» Adjusting your voice and tonality to match the present moment

» Pause

» Be a man (or woman) of your word

» Be memorable for the right reasons!

These are just a few of the things that should be practiced while interacting with another person.

Concepts like these are extremely vital to a millennials future success. Anyone can instantly gain respect and influence by enhancing these types of skills.

Internet

It's obvious now that people need to put a filter on what they publish and send online. Most people have regretted sending or posting something at one point in their lives. Although the Internet has propelled our society forward, it has created a new little world of disasters waiting to happen. Here are a few T.I.P's on how to use the Internet for millennials and the companies that surround them:

» Monitor usage – It's easy to start slipping into a black hole on any website. Become self-aware of how much time is being spent on the Internet and where it's being wasted.

» Create scripts – If employees are sending out the same three emails to customers on a daily basis, creating scripts will save time and streamline the process. The ability to create quality website, email, and marketing copy will increase conversion and efficiency.

» Use discretion – If you wouldn't want your mom or boss to see that post, then it's probably best you don't post it. People get fired every day for posting things online that they shouldn't have. If you have to second guess yourself, it's a bad idea.

» Leverage search engines – The Internet is the most powerful source of information in the world. If you don't have the answer, a website probably does. Search for that content and learn from others. Resourcefulness beats a lack of it 10 times out of 10.

» Safety first – Once your password is in the possession of a hacker, your fate is in their hands.

Cautiously download, and remember that there is a dark side to the web. Millennials have been trained to understand the importance of protecting their information. Evil tends to take advantage of the naiveté of others.

Phone

Millennials tend to be great communicators via text, but lack enthusiasm when it comes to phone calls. Phone calls can make or break our careers. We've all had a few big ones, and they can be nerve-racking at times. Having great phone skills is one of the quickest ways to propel anyone's career forward. We must remember that no one can see us on the other end. So, the way we speak is that much more important. Here are a few phone etiquette T.I.P's for the 21st century.

» Tonality – The inflections in your voice become increasingly important because you're not face-to-face. The way your voice moves up and down, loud and soft, questioning and answering matters a lot. Make sure you're always conscious of your tonality and how it affects your conversations moving forward.

» Intro and exit – As someone who had a stutter, this is something I previously struggled with. The primary and recency effect says people remember the beginning and the end of most things; the middle just seems to blend in. Become great at getting the ball rolling in a conversation and knowing how and when to close it out. "People will forget what you said, people will forget what you did, but people will never forget how you made them feel " – Maya Angelou.

» Body – I know it seems counterintuitive, but how you use your body while speaking on the phone can help or hurt you. I typically like to be standing up with my shoulders back, preferably walking either in circles or down a path. Walking keeps my mind moving. Some people like sitting at their desk with their feet kicked up. Whatever makes you the best version of yourself is what you should do. Don't negate your physiology just because others can't see it. Some may still be able to hear it.

» Distractions – It's easy to get distracted while on the phone. Your sight, taste, touch, smell and half your hearing is in one place. The other half of your hearing is in another place. It's easy to get preoccupied with the Internet or other interruptions while on the phone, but it's a slippery slope that can get you into trouble. Focus on the task at hand and complete it with vigor. Then, move on to whatever else you have to do. Stop trying to kill two birds with one stone.

Managers should be *TIP*-ing each of their subordinates once a week at minimum. If you're in a virtual company, then double down on the I (internet) and the P (phone) since in person communication isn't feasible. Realize that this is just as applicable for customers as it is for employees, coworkers and anyone else you happen to meet. There is no excuse for not properly communicating in today's business world. Good communication is about adapting to the style of the person you're speaking with. Millennials need to be properly trained on how to communicate in society if they want to thrive in a multi-generational workforce. However, no matter how advanced society gets, communication will always be the cornerstone of our civilization and its growth.

Eisenhauer, T. (n.d.). How to Communicate with Millennials at Work 23 Surefire Tips to Retire the Stereotypes. Retrieved January, 2017, from https://axerosolutions.com/blogs/timeisenhauer/pulse

/307/how-to-communicate-with-millennials-at-work-23-surefire-tips-to-retire-the-stereotypes

■ Outside the Office

To fully engage millennials, interactions outside the office are a must. People you work with need to realize that you're more than a role (or job title); you're an individual. You're a human, you know – the type with a personality, a family, and a favorite sports team.

Managers need to be able to relate with millennials both personally and professionally in today's business environment. Doing so requires people to show their true colors. How else can we expect to gain the trust of our peers? They need to know the man (or woman) behind the mask.

It's the responsibility of the company, as well as the managers, to actively engage the employee outside the office. We've already talked about happy hours and field trips, but what about volunteer work?

Volunteering to support a cause shows a collective effort from all who choose to participate. Maybe it's a charity golf event? Even if you don't play golf, just go to drive around the golf cart – it's the best part anyway! The group's ability to connect outside the office will make them more collaborative inside the office.

There's something to be said for leaving all the office work behind to work together and do something different. The only time we typically see co-workers is when there is work to be done. We spend 40 hours a week with these people, yet we don't have the opportunity to get to know them outside of their role. Fortunately, times have changed.

Interacting outside the office builds trust and teamwork. It strengthens relationships and encourages employees to care about each other's overall well-being. Millennials want to enjoy the presence of the people they work with. If the only interactions between employees are only during work hours, millennials will start to associate "the team" to "work." Companies need to find ways to engage this generation outside office so that "the team" is associated with "fun."

The workplace no longer represents a place that's sole purpose is to create a profit. Older generations tend to look at the office as a place that's *only* for work. They don't have as much of an interest in hanging out with co-workers outside of the office. In today's world, the company we work for now represents our beliefs, our purpose, our interests and for some people, our best friends.

If you're going to spend 40 hours a week with millennials, it's important you know who they are, not just what they do. If you want to create an enjoyable workplace inside the company, start getting creative and designing some magical moments.

■ Ongoing Conversations

The concept of annual reviews still baffles me to this day.

It's an event that an employee gets all worked up for. They're hoping that for the past year they have lived up to the company standards, and that they're worth a measly 2% raise.

It's a joke.

What millennials want to see implemented in every office are ongoing conversations. You know, the ones to make sure we're still on the right track. There is no reason in the 21st century why companies should be doing annual reviews. If you feel it's necessary, have a large review each quarter. In reality, we should be having a weekly conversation with our bosses about performance, improvements and struggles. The more often we go through this process, the better off we all are. The best way to stay on the same page is to create an ongoing conversation. They help us become self-aware and focus on exactly what needs to be done. We're not asking to be coddled for eight hours a day. We're asking for open and transparent communication.

There is an analogy from the technology movement that shows the power of ongoing conversations. In the tech world, there's a concept called iterative design.

"Iterative design is an approach of incrementally developing and refining a design based on feedback and evaluation." – InstructionalDesign.org

Iterative design is a rapid prototyping process that developers use to create the best product in the shortest amount of time. It's a feedback loop that allows for constant and never ending improvement. This progress is based on communication with both teammates and customers to help further develop the idea or system that's being implemented.

This same concept needs to be used within the office when speaking with millennials. Constructive criticism is what has allowed me to propel my career so quickly. When my TEDx Talk came out, I didn't try to make it go viral. I sent it to every public speaker and CEO I was connected to and asked them to critique the performance. No sugar-coated bullshit. I wanted the cold hard truth. Welcoming constructive criticism is what allowed me to exponentially improve my stage presence in a short period of time. My outreach efforts were a form of iterative design, and helped me obtain feedback in the most efficient way possible. We can't be afraid of our mistakes if we're looking to grow. We must embrace them so we know where and how to improve when we move forward. All of this starts with an ongoing conversation.

Millennials look to keep conversations open within the organization. Keeping an open dialogue on the team promotes a culture of honesty. It keeps the lines of communication open, and it allows for a feedback loop to increase performance. No matter how great a company is, it can always get better. Keeping open conversations is the quickest way to uncover problems and develop solutions.

■ Integrity and Respect

I n a vain world, integrity and respect have become valuable commodities. As individualist thinkers, there's no doubt that this generation puts their own well-being above others. That's not a bad thing, if we uphold integrity and respect while doing so.

One of the first books I read after college was called *The 4 Agreements*. It's a very quick read, and the first agreement is to always "be a man (or woman) of your word." I've encountered too many business professionals who don't approach situations with integrity.

I once worked at an organization that told me I would have my birthday off in the employment documents that I signed when I was hired. When I blocked October 6th off a week beforehand, I was ridiculed for doing so. I wasn't frustrated because I had to work on my birthday. I was confused because the documents I signed said one thing, and my boss completely ignored what I thought to be "the policy." The way it was communicated was extremely abrasive and it made me question the integrity and congruency of the organization. I felt it not only lacked integrity, but it was also disrespectful. In hindsight, there were certainly things I could have done to avoid a confrontation like this. But, hindsight's 20/20. It was a minor problem that gave me great insight about the company's communication and culture.

If we want our employees to respect us, we must respect them. Employers who feel that they are entitled to respect have no business employing anybody. Many managers feel that they are entitled to respect because their job title says so. This is not the case for true leaders. They realize that respect is grown through integrity. The situation with my old boss would have turned out differently if he had approached the situation from a place of understanding.

You get respect for what you do, not what you say you do. Do you respect an asshole that's a millionaire? Or a guy who makes $50K per year, but always offers a helping hand around the neighborhood? We tend to respect the person who respects us back.

If you demand respect, you're probably the type of person who couldn't get it otherwise. Your job doesn't give you respect; your actions do. Managers have a hard time realizing this; leaders don't.

Twenty-first century business is based on trust. People buy products from companies they trust and look for jobs from organizations they trust. So, if you want to employ and sell to millennials, you need to trust them. If you don't trust them, they won't trust you. If you don't respect them, they won't respect you. If they don't respect or trust you, good luck doing business with them!

If management helps employees succeed, they will help the company succeed. It seems pretty obvious, right? The sad reality is that what managers (or anyone for that matter) say versus what they do are two completely different realities.

Millennials want to work with management on equal terms. We're excited about working with older generations, but only if the relationship is on equal terms with mutual respect (1). To expect respect and talk down to a millennial will get managers nowhere. Older generations sometimes feel as if they've earned respect because they've "been in the biz for 40 years." But, it seems like people who have been in the biz for that long tend to assume admiration for all their efforts. They assume they know all the answers because they've been around the block. Sometimes that overconfidence in knowledge can bite the smartest people in the butt.

A millennial has no problem respecting authority if it's implemented in a way that's empowering. I frequently hear that managers are frustrated with millennials who lack respect. In today's world, you can't expect respect; you must create it.

If you want to create loyalty, you need to get a millennial to open up. They need to be comfortable expressing themselves freely and see that collaboration is something that's encouraged, not frowned upon. Millennials want to see that they're treated as an equal, and that their vision matters just as much as anyone else's. They want to know that management will be transparent with them, and give them the professional courtesy to be open and honest when there is a problem.

Most companies don't do any of those things. They say they do in their company mission, but they don't act on it. As we said, respect is based off your actions, not your words. Not being a man (or company) of your word just results in bad blood and disrespect. Unfortunately, disrespect results in disengagement and a lack of productivity. A lack of respect and integrity creates a downward spiral for all of those involved.

Here's the bottom line: if you want a millennial to respect you or your business, you need to create attachment. Get them to believe in your cause and mission. It's easy to quit a job. It's impossible to abort a mission.

Respect shouldn't only be a part of your culture; it should be a part of your thoughts, feelings and actions. Integrity and respect is what will turn you from the influenced to the influencer.

Millennials or Generation Y, Who They Are and Why They're Hated. (2013, June 05). Retrieved January, 2017, from
https://www.youtube.com/watch?v=jHpbdQCMnwQ

■ Trust

Trust – we either have it or we don't. When we first meet someone, we base trust on our instinct or gut feeling. Trust happens deep within our brain in an area called our limbic system. If you haven't watched Simon Sinek's TEDx *Start With Why,* I advise you to take an 18-minute break and watch it (1).

Watching Simon's talk is what motivated me to do mine. I would never suggest putting my book down for someone else's content if I didn't really think that it would make a difference in your life. To understand trust, we must understand the basic constructs of the human brain.

We trust those from our past. We trust those that have interests tied to our own. But, who should we trust the most? Ourselves.

Too often in life we doubt ourselves. It seems like inadequate people tend to have tons of confidence in themselves, while the smart ones are full of doubt. It's time to change that story.

"You have to trust in something – your gut, destiny, life, karma, whatever. This approach has never let me down, and it has made all the difference in my life." – Steve Jobs

That quote really hit home for me. I used to trust everyone, and thought that everyone had my best interest in mind. That's far from the truth.

In a world where your words can be screenshotted or recorded, only to be put online moments later, we must be increasingly careful of who we let into our world.

This ties in beautifully with corporate culture. If managers want to be trusted by their millennial cohorts, they need to be a human, not a robot. The real world isn't all reports and numbers, it's emotion. If you're the boss who's looking at the numbers and wondering, "Why isn't the team performing?" Ding. Ding. Ding. We have an answer! Look in the mirror.

Humans are emotional creatures. If you're not connecting on an emotional level to your co-workers, find a way to do so ASAP. Take them out for a beer after work. Go out to lunch with the millennials that report to you. Listen to them. Walk a day in their shoes. Who knows? You may learn something.

There is nothing worse than a baby boomer who thinks they have nothing to learn from a millennial. Trust me.

Vice versa is also true; millennials can't be up on their high horse and think that they know it all just because "we're in tune with what's actually going on today." That's not how the world works. It's called *The Millennial Merger* for a reason. We need to merge ideologies. We need to come from a place of understanding and appreciation for one another. We need to have a merging of the minds, and we need to listen and think before we act. That's how trust is created. That's how success is created. And, that's how you create a dynamic workplace that will thrive for years to come.

Our entire capitalistic free-enterprise system is built on trust. Our economy is literally standing on a support system, and that system is called trust. Our economy is comprised of a network of people creating mutually beneficial exchanges of goods and services. Trust is the lubricant that makes it all work (2). Economists measure our economy by GDP (gross domestic product), but the exchange of dollars is directly tied to trust. Trust is tied to consumer confidence, and consumer confidence is a measurement of how willing people are to spend their money. It's a never-ending vicious circle. Trust is part of that invisible ROI (return on investment) we spoke about earlier.

Millennials don't want to be micromanaged; they want to be trusted. On the flip side, employers don't want to be second-guessed; they want the same type of trust employees want. Baby boomers want trust to be earned and not given, and millennials want to be trusted in order to trust another. It's a flawed system.

Inevitably, technology will get more advanced and people will become more skeptical of who they trust. Over the next few decades, there will be a constant trust-battle between generations. However, once the organization creates trust between management, employees, and customers, the magic you've been working toward will appear, loud and clear.

Sinek, S. (2009, September). How great leaders inspire action. Retrieved January, 2017, from https://www.ted.com/talks/simon_sinek_how_great_le aders_inspire_action

Corning, P. (2011, October 24). The Value of Trust. Retrieved January, 2017, from https://www.psychologytoday.com/blog/the-fair-society/201110/the-value-trust

■ Supporting Causes

This is one of the largest fundamental shifts we've seen so far in 21st century business. Supporting a cause, whether it be a nonprofit, or a community, or a movement, has traditionally been looked at as an afterthought. "After we get all of our work done (and make all of our money), then we'll spend a few minutes helping out a cause... but only if we have some extra time." That was the old way of thinking, but millennials are changing this thought process. Today's great companies are using their time, money and energy to support causes that are making a difference.

Your company (or even you as an individual) needs to find something bigger than business to believe in. Maybe it's a cause that's near and dear to your heart, maybe it affects a loved one, maybe it affects your business, or maybe it affects your nation. <u>However, there's always something to stand for, and in today's world, if you don't stand for something, you stand for nothing</u>.

This generation isn't here to fulfill your mission statement or to bring home a paycheck. They're here to enjoy life and make a difference while they're at it. Since the beginning of time, we've gauged a company's success based on the numbers. Although that may hold true for investors and shareholders, it doesn't work long-term for employees and customers.

The people surrounding your business want to see that you care about something more than money. Business is about helping people. The more people you help, the more successful you become. It's really that simple.

Supporting causes has opened a whole new world of opportunity for social entrepreneurship. This generation doesn't value money as highly as other generations (at least not yet). They value experiences, helping people, magical moments, friendship, connection and collaboration. Your company's activities need to align with those types of values if you want to do business with the millennial generation. The best way to do that is to support a cause and stand up for what you believe in. This is the new evolution of capitalism; a more socially focused entity driven by a cause.

I learned something else very valuable from Michael Houlihan. When starting up Barefoot Wines, Michael came up with a concept called "worthy-cause marketing." At first I was skeptical, but he told me some stories that blew my mind. Worthy-cause marketing is the concept of leveraging your product or service within a specific cause or community, and then blitzing that market with value added experiences. Michael typically donated wine to fundraisers and other community events. They would set up a table and talk to customers during these events. He would typically be listed as one of the main sponsors. Michael and his wife, Bonnie, would ask customers for their opinion and work to connect with the community in that city. This helped them build a relationship with the community at large and gain feedback while doing so. Being a part of the local community made it easier for Barefoot Wines to place their products in local liquor stores and super markets.

The whole concept of worthy-cause marketing is to get creative with how you help others, engage in the community, and show off your business. Aligning your values with the community in a way that allows you to help others and promote your product is a win-win for everyone. Just going for a quick sales pitch doesn't work anymore. If the only value you're getting is the bigger numbers in your bank account, your glory may be short-lived.

Finding a non-profit to support could even turn into a strategic partnership down the road. If you are wondering what cause or charity could best serve your company, you could benefit from reverse engineering your own business model. The first question to start with should be, "Who are my customers?" Once you've properly identified your customer base, you can go find a non-profit with that exact same user base. Properly aligning with that cause will give you more access to your target demographic.

Every company is in the business of generating leads and building relationships. You can look at supporting causes as an effective lead generation strategy. If you and a potential lead are supporting the same cause, you have something in common and can now go about building rapport. Creating a relationship never seemed so easy, right?

A word of caution though: if you're only supporting a cause to generate leads, you're not thinking about this the right way. You want to find a cause that you (and your company) believe in. My purpose here was just to show you how supporting causes can be profitable in terms of how you spend your time, money and energy.

If you only think of your marketing budget in terms of advertising, you'll lose to those who are getting creative. Today, your marketing budget can be used to help change the world and make money while doing it. Millennials want to support causes and connect with the people they're affecting. Companies need to start getting concerned about how they can make a difference in this world by supporting something they believe in. Eventually the money will come.

" A hero is someone who has given his or her life to something bigger than oneself."

Joseph Campbell

■ Compensation and Benefits

All the baby boomers are freaking out because compensation is a huge topic with millennials right now. I have received many calls from people saying things like, "Jesse, I don't know how to get these millennials on board – they don't want my money." That may be true, at least for the time being.

As millennials age, we will inevitably value money, at least more so than we do today. When we have a spouse, kids and a mortgage, we will need money. That's just a reality of life. But overall, millennials just don't care as much about money as our predecessors. If anything, this should be good news for every company that employs millennials! This gives companies an opportunity to spend that extra money on creating a culture that lasts much longer than any product or pay check.

Money comes and goes, but how someone feels when they walk in the office lasts forever. Here are a few things to consider when offering compensation packages and benefits to millennial prospects:

» Travel / time off – Since this generation tends to value traveling experiences, management could offer reimbursement of a domestic or international plane ticket (even if it's half).

» Culture – Little things like dress attire, shorter Fridays during the summer, lunch with the CEO on your birthday, and telecommuting tell an employee that you're flexible and always looking out for their best interest.

» Impact – Businesses today have a social responsibility. Offer employees time off for volunteering or match their donations to charity. Working for a cause beats working for a profit.

» Insurances – Make sure your employees are properly protected. If insurance is left solely on the employee, it may take up a significant portion of their income. Insurance plus taxes plus all the other fees in life don't leave much for disposable income. Lend a helping hand when it comes to insurance. Employees have grown to expect it.

» Training – I don't want to beat the dead horse, but helping someone achieve both personal and professional growth will have them hooked! Self-development is about moving forward as an individual. If you help them do that, they'll help you make a profit.

» Chill Rooms – Offer an area within the office where work is off limits. Work can get stressful. It helps to have a "zen" area where people can tune out for a few minutes.

» Community involvement – Offering to pay for things like chamber of commerce fees is a great incentive. It costs you a few hundred bucks, it develops their network, and it gives them an opportunity to get you new business!

» Other experiences – Sending employees to conferences and trade shows is a great way to give them a new experience. It can help the company and the individual grow at the same time!

» Stock – Don't be greedy with stock. Every company should have a 10% employee stock option pool (ESOP) at minimum. Your employees are helping you grow; they deserve a piece of the pie.

» Food – As corny as it sounds, free food makes life just a little easier. Buying lunch (or bringing it to the office) can add up. Even providing snacks can put smiles on employee's faces every day. I've also heard of companies that do monthly potlucks at the office. It's hard to have a frown when there is food in front of your face!

» Fitness – This generation cares a lot more about health than our predecessors. Reimbursement for gym memberships (or providing one) will go a long way for personal growth and productivity.

» Tickets – Sporting events. Concerts. Cruises. The county fair. It doesn't matter. Use tickets to events to spice up the workplace. These can be used as incentives for top performers or as monthly reminders of how much you care.

» Discounted services – Things like dry cleaning pickup, car washes and oil changes from the comfort of your office save employee's time. No one wants to go run a ton of errands after work. They just want to relax. I've even seen companies that have partnerships to help their employees receive discounts for technology purchases and local organizations. Start getting creative!

» Choices – I get it. It may not be possible to provide all these benefits. Let employees pick and choose a few from a list. Giving millennials a choice on the benefits they want allows them to choose based on their values.

The realm of thinking that compensation and benefits are directly tied to money needs to be thrown out the window. You may not be able to compete with Fortune 500 companies on salary, but you can on benefits. Start thinking outside the box and recognize that the best benefits are the ones that will align with a millennials values. If you're aligning with their values, you'll be able to provide benefits that will make your organization stand out from the crowd.

Benefits need to be thought of not only as a retention tool, but as a growth tool. The freedom for millennials to be creative, have access to executives, and give feedback and mentorship are all free. They create a culture of transparency and communication within the office, and they don't cost you a dime. You're investing in your employees in one of three ways: time, money and energy. The goal of this investment is to make sure that employees are experiencing growth, because if they're growing, the company is growing. It's a simple cause and effect.

What You Ought to Know

■ Marketing

A majority of this book is really about how to market to millennials, both customers and employees alike. Today's marketing is about empathizing and understanding the needs of the client. Organizations have to start a conversation, align their values, engage the customer, and create a great user experience.

We can notice most of these concepts in advertisements and sales pitches. The products and services companies provide are there to solve a certain need – the need to either move away from pain or toward pleasure. Simply put, our brain's job is to minimize pain and maximize pleasure (1). Unfortunately, since pain tends to be more immediate, we concentrate on avoiding it at all costs. Most advertisements will show you how not purchasing will cause massive amounts of pain, and buying will cause massive amounts of pleasure. Today's marketing is based on consumer behavior, analytics, and most importantly, human psychology. Organizations will continue to use these principles to get consumers to purchase their products regardless of generational differences.

Pain is the most powerful motivator of all; that's just how the human brain works. However, I caution people to be extremely careful with this principle. Millennials aren't going to buy products after watching commercials that make them feel like complete shit. It's okay to show us a little of the darkness, but focus on the light and how our lives will be better with your company by our side. Millennials look at our purchasing decisions as a partnership, and no one wants to partner up with a "Negative Nancy."

If you want to be great at marketing in the 21st century become the light in someone's life. Create a brand that consumers want to bring up during conversation. Word of mouth marketing is still the most powerful mover in purchasing decisions (2). Your marketing can make me feel unbearable amounts of pain, but if I don't see the pleasure I'll get from purchasing, I'm not going to buy your product. It's important in today's marketing to paint both sides of the picture. Show us how we'll experience massive pain from not buying your product and massive pleasure from taking out our credit card.

However, as users start to consume, they inevitably paint their own picture. When a product is released, it's up to the company to get the word out. But as a product penetrates the market, it's the consumers who are going to paint the real picture, whether companies like it or not. The way organizations market their product is what sets up the expectations for the experience. It's really the consumers who create the brand identity long-term; the companies are just there to facilitate the changes along the way.

In today's world, if companies are selling technology, it's expected to work. We're a mobile and social generation that thrives on instant gratification, and we're constantly communicating with others. If your marketing strategy directly aligns with how we use technology, then you'll come off as relatable.

A company's marketing efforts should always be authentic and transparent. We live in a digital world where fact checking can take place in 30 seconds or less.

If an organization lies in their marketing, they will get exposed, they will be called out, and their name will be tarnished accordingly.

Organizations must make a commitment to market the company in an ethical way, but also in a way that will turn heads. We live in a viral society where one online video can literally change the landscape of any business.

When marketing, it's important to focus on the experience your offering creates. <u>Experiences create emotions, and emotions spend money</u>. People tend to make their purchasing decisions based on emotional reasons and rationalize it with logic. Most of you can probably recall a time when a salesman asked you the question, "How does that make you feel?" All humans want is a certain feeling, so make sure your marketing shows the emotional advantages of your product or service. All humans desire the positive emotional states they value the highest.

Marketing is about paying attention and listening to the needs of the consumer. Marketing is about supporting the sales process. And most importantly, marketing to millennials is about realizing that one size does not fit all. <u>If you listen to our voices, you won't hear a generation; you'll hear individuals</u>. You won't be able to make every individual happy always and forever; that's not realistic. What is realistic is listening to your consumers. They may tell you something that could change the world.

Grossman, S. (n.d.). Reinforcing Effects of Electrical Brain Stimulation. Retrieved January, 2017, from https://www.wireheading.com/brainstim/

Association, W. O. (n.d.). Marketers Say "Word of Mouth Marketing" Is More Effective than Traditional Marketing; Forecast Big Increase in Social Media Spending. Retrieved January, 2017, from

http://www.prnewswire.com/news-releases/marketers-say-word-of-mouth-marketing-is-more-effective-than-traditional-marketing-forecast-big-increase-in-social-media-spending-232486271.html

■ Social Media

This is one of the more profound double-edged topics of this book. Social media has helped our society and generation in so many ways, while at the same time, given a platform for ignorance and stupidity.

People tend to post on social media because it makes them feel *significant*. It makes them feel heard and loved. Isn't that all we want in this world? Love? People want to feel like they are cared about; they want to feel a connection. Posting on social media makes us feel important, and if just one person is impacted by our post, we get a feeling of prominence. However, there's no doubt in anyone's mind that this industry has caused a different type of narcissism our society has never seen before.

The social movement has permanently stained our society, both in good and bad ways. Social media's trickledown effect has impacted gaming, dating, reviewing, and how people buy and sell products. Most websites will now allow people to sign in with one of their social media accounts. It allows them to scrape your data and study your interests. Why has the social media movement created so much controversy?

Baby boomers look at social media as a distraction in the workplace, while millennials look at it as a leverage point. Social media platforms produce a ton of noise, but some of that noise is applicable to you. It's just about sorting through the shit to get to the gold.

There's an old saying, "content is king," but the way we now measure the effectiveness of that content is through likes, shares, comments, headlines and controversies on social media. The content king is now measured predominantly through social metrics instead of just "views." I constantly find myself saying things like, "How in the world did this become a trending topic?" or "What has our society come to?" The trending topics on social sites never cease to amaze me. Social media has given the ignorant a platform to spread their bigotry, and given the influential a platform to create significant societal advances.

Social media has fundamentally changed the way we communicate as a society. The largest media corporation in the world today (Facebook) doesn't produce any media (1). They simply provide a platform for others to share their thoughts. It was an ingenious idea that had most people saying, "Why didn't I think of that?" With competition brewing, Facebook will soon start creating content of their own."

Social media has changed political campaigns, marketing, holidays, and how we mourn the loss of others. It has created a more interconnected world, but also created an addiction. <u>We have become more connected with the world around us, but less connected with ourselves.</u> When the present moment doesn't appeal to us anymore, we find social media to be a comforting distraction. The problem is, we tend to compare our real lives to everyone else's highlight reels (2). Most people only post their best moments, leaving users feeling inadequate while vicariously living though the superficial lives of others.

Social Media Anxiety Disorder is now researched and has been shown to cause depression, a feeling of inadequacy, inferiority and embarrassment. Social Anxiety Disorder (the parent of Social Media Anxiety

Disorder) is now the third leading psychological disorder in the U.S. (3). These disorders are real, and can lead to drug abuse and depression. These disorders are in their infancy and the more we study them, the more we'll understand the impact of social media on the human brain.

Ask yourselves, "If social media didn't exist today, what would I use the internet for?" Besides Google, there aren't many sites that I frequently visit that don't have some sort of social aspect. Unless we're researching something specific, I'd argue that most people feel the same way.

Social media has been a part of our generation since childhood, and will continue to affect us for the foreseeable future. I'm not here to give you social media tips and tricks. Statistics are forever changing and good advice today is bad advice tomorrow. Just know that this industry is a part of our society whether you like it or not. Accept it, leverage it and help change the lives of those who use it.

McRae, H. (n.d.). Facebook, Airbnb, Uber, and the unstoppable rise of the content non-generators. Retrieved January, 2017, from http://www.independent.co.uk/news/business/comment/hamish-mcrae/facebook-airbnb-uber-and-the-unstoppable-rise-of-the-content-non-generators-10227207.html

Steers, M.-L. N., Wickham, R. E., & Acitelli, L. K. (2014). Seeing everyone else's highlight reels: How Facebook usage is linked to depressive symptoms. Journal of Social and Clinical Psychology, 33(8), 701. doi:

Social Media Anxiety Disorder|Causes|Symptoms|Treatment|Recovery Tips. (2016, July 05). Retrieved January, 2017, from http://www.epainassist.com/mental-health/social-media-anxiety-disorder

Why use Social Media?

"Marketing is no longer about the stuff that you make, but about the stories you tell."

- Seth Godin

■ Buying Patterns

Many millennials have a minimalist mentality (1). I bet you can't say that 10 times fast.

The fact is, millennials don't purchase as much as you want them too. We've witnessed American consumerism turn bad and because of that, have adopted an uncluttered lifestyle. The simple life leads millennials to purchase emotional states. Millennials desire the experience and the moment – that's what we're really purchasing.

There are many types of people who will buy your product:

» People with similar values.

» People who have a problem (pain) that you can solve.

» People who stand for what you believe in.

» People who have heard your message.

» People who dislike your competition.

» People who get pleasure from your product / service.

» People who have friends that use your product / service.

» People who feel that your value exceeds your price.

» People who like you.

Can people that don't fit those criteria still buy from you? Of course, but it's a good starting point for discovering and marketing to the right people as effectively as possible. If your target market is not millennials today, it will be in the near future. You can only avoid us for so long.

When millennials are making purchasing decisions, they're doing it from people they trust. Business is now primarily based off relationships, not transactions. Customers want to keep an open dialogue and get to know the business (or their employees) on a personal level.

Our generation is especially price sensitive as we try to chip away at our student loan debt. If value is not greater than price, don't bother trying to sell to millennials. The profit margins in retail have become razor thin because of the internet's level playing field. This has changed the competitive landscape so that the small guys can compete. With modern advertising, organizations can target a user based on any given metric within their digital footprint.

Millennials prefer to shop from a mobile device, at any time, and in any place. Ironically, we use social media for a lot of our shopping information. What our friends have to say about a business speaks volumes to us as consumers. We also want to engage with brands on social media and see them respond to us. What a concept!

Even when we go shopping in a mall, we tend to use sites like Google and Amazon to compare prices. If we can find the same product for cheaper online, your store just served as a playground to test out products. It's one of the unfortunate truths of 21st century consumerism.

With the rise of ecommerce, our society has experienced cybersecurity risks. Things like identity fraud and phishing scams have become more popular in recent years. There's nothing worse than feeling loyal to a brand that gives up your credit information to hackers. Because of this, many millennials would prefer to use gift cards or PayPal (2). Loyalty programs can be a hit with millennial consumers, but only if there's legitimate value added. A loyalty program with no perks is just a waste of time and space in our wallets.

Very few people in this generation are influenced by traditional advertising. Recorded TV shows and ad blockers for Internet browsers have taken a lot of the clutter out of our day to day lives. Very few people go out and buy a product because they saw your ad. Companies are always vying for our attention, but truth be told, many of these companies just advertise to stay relevant.

Most importantly, millennial customers want to work with a company to create new products. Writing a bad review doesn't mean we're going to stop buying. It means we care enough to let your company know that we want to see these improvements (so we can continue to buy your products). We want to be involved in the innovation process. Collaborate with us. Ask us. Develop with us. And maybe if you're lucky, you can sell some more products to us.

The Johnny Rockets restaurant chain recently went through a brand shift to appeal to millennials. "Every detail about the development of Johnny's Burger Factory, from the first design to construction, product development and marketing had a new kind of consumer in mind. It's not possible to ignore millennials and still be competitive in the better burger category," Johnny Rockets CEO Charles Bruce said (3). Even older, more established brands are taking notice that millennials are changing the way people consume products.

Sales is a transfer of emotion, and one of the emotions that consumers want is certainty. Certainty that your product will work, that it's valuable, that it will solve their problems and that it will give them pleasure. That's it. Every consumer wants to think that they're buying because it was logical, but they're all lying to themselves. Consumers take out their wallets when a product satisfies a certain emotional need.

It doesn't matter if they're male, female, millennial, boomer, black, white or upside down. They're buying because it feels good. Understanding the emotional needs and desires of a target market will give organizations the insight they need to acquire new customers.

The Fall Of Materialism: Why More Millennials Aspire To Have Nothing. (2015, November 18). Retrieved January, 2017, from http://elitedaily.com/life/culture/millennials-minimalists/1256085/

Electronic gift cards gaining popularity among millennials. (2014, November 20). Retrieved January, 2017, from http://www.cbsnews.com/news/electronic-gift-cards-gaining-popularity-among-millennials/

Johnny Rockets Opens Millennials Concept. (2015, November 11). Retrieved January, 2017, from http://burgerbusiness.com/johnny-rockets-opens-millennials-concept/

"Knowing who your customers are is great, but knowing how they behave is even better."
—Jon Miller

The Millennial Dictionary

Two millennials walk in a bar.

One of those millennials happens to bump into the other millennial that's walking out the door. To no one's surprise, they're both looking down at their phones. Here's how the conversation goes.

Guy #1 – Sorry, dude.

Guy #2 – My bad, man.

Guy #1 – No worries, you're good.

Guy #2 – What's up? I couldn't hear you.

Guy #1 – I said, no worries.

Guy #2 – All good, man. Have a good one.

If that conversation didn't amuse you, it's probably because you're a millennial. If you got a giggle out of it, you realize the way this generation communicates can be absolutely insane at times.

I didn't realize the way we communicated was off-putting until one of my mentors called me out on it. He told me to stop using the phrases "What's up?" when clarifying a statement and "My bad." This got me into some research on other things millennials say that others question.

I'm warning you now that what you're about to read may feel like nails on a chalkboard:

» *Sorrynotsorry* – Both an incomplete sentence and thought.

» *On fleek* – On point or excellent.

» *I can't even* – Another incomplete sentence and thought.

» *The struggle is real* – I used to date a girl that had this as her go-to saying. Great girl, but needless to say, that relationship didn't last long.

» *B.A.E.* – Which means "Before anyone else." It's typically used to describe someone's significant other (instead of the word 'babe').

» *Perf* – Perfect – This one is just an abbreviation, mostly used by girls.

» *J.K.* – Just kidding – This is commonly used across other generations.

» *T.B.H.* – To be honest – It's a way for millennials to confront controversial issues without becoming abrasive.

» *G.O.A.T.* – Greatest of All Time – This one is acceptable across all generations. It's typically used when referring to athletes, or just all around awesome people. Tom Brady, he's the GOAT!

» *Netflix and Chill* – This is one of those terms boomers take literally. This term was brought to light by men who wanted to invite women over for a sexual encounter, but use this phrase instead of calling the interaction at face value. They thought they were slick by asking their counterpart to come over and have a "Netflix and Chill" night.

» *Y.O.L.O.* – You Only Live Once – When this term was coined, it promoted stupid people doing even stupider things because... YOLO! Recently, I've actually heard successful business men from the Gen X community use it to describe going after business deals and pushing the limit. The concept behind the acronym is solid, but only if it's used in situations of growth, not decay.

» *F.O.M.O.* – "Fear of Missing Out" – Social media has perpetuated this phenomenon. Watching all your friends post pictures of an event while you're sick at home can cause some serious FOMO.

» *YAS* – Like Yes – Except a more extreme type of approval.

» *Turnt* – Drunk.

» *N.S.A.* – "No Strings Attached."

» *N.S.F.W.* – "Not Safe for Work."

» *Throw Shade* – to show disapproval or trash talk.

» *Thirsty* – Desperately seeking the attention of others. At first, this term was used for dating purposes, but today I hear business people using it while referring to customers, sales people, and potential new hires. If you're thirsty, you've lost all leverage. Don't be the thirsty one.

I truly hope that in 20 years, we will look at this list and be disgusted with ourselves (at least with most of these sayings). The terminology almost sounds like another dialect of English, or maybe a communication medium from a less advanced society. I'm not sure. All I know is when boomers hear words like these, they scratch their heads and say, "Kids these days."

No one knows whether these words are just fads, or if they'll stay a part of our culture moving forward. It's not important that other generations adopt this lingo. But it is important that other generations understand modern terminology as it grows and progresses. Although millennials are not the first generation to abbreviate words and sayings, it will be interesting to see how this trend progresses over time.

These sayings tend to perpetuate negative connotations to this generation, but it makes you wonder, what other words will be popular in future generations? I'm sure there were words from the 1900's that were once popular, but are now extinct. Although many of these sayings irk previous generations, we must always remember that the words we use are a byproduct of the moments we experience.

■ Weakness

J ust like many things in history, this generation's strength is our biggest weakness. Millennials define many of our strengths based around technology, but it's also our Achilles' heel. Moore's Law says that our processing power doubles every two years (1). This allows us to obtain and create information quicker and quicker every day. Instant gratification and expectations encapsulate our weaknesses and solidify our strengths.

However, this age of technology has brought to light this culture of instant gratification. Do you have a problem? There's an app or website that most likely solves your pain. God forbid there's not. This generation has a hard time waiting. We're used to all of our resources being within arm's reach.

This instant gratification ideology has devalued face-to-face communication. Why go talk to people when we can FaceTime, call, text, Skype, etc.? To many millennials, there's no point.

Instant gratification is the evil twin to the much less desirable delayed gratification. I graduated with a degree in entrepreneurship. The two things my professor, Dr. Dever, instilled in me from day one was that <u>successful entrepreneurs have two key skills: delayed gratification and opportunity recognition</u>. He is a baby boomer and he is right. Our generation is so caught up in the instant lifestyle that it seems absurd to delay satisfaction for another time. If you want to be a successful business person, you need to work today for a better tomorrow. That will never change.

Instant gratification has caused this generation to suffer from career impatience. We want to be happy in our job and we want to be happy now. Although it may take time for employers to assimilate to this generation, it's important that millennials not get too hasty with job hunting. We don't have the patience for stagnation, which results in unrealistic upward mobility expectations.

To be satisfied in this moment, we tend to want the ability to do what we want, when we want to do it. Technology gives us the belief that work can get done anytime and anywhere, hence our need for work-life integration. That statement is true, but the fact that we expect instantaneous satisfaction is what annoys previous generations. When things are expected, it shows a sense of entitlement. I quoted Frank Underwood in my TEDx Talk, and I'll quote him again here, "You are entitled to nothing" (Spacey, *2013*).

Entitlement can cause huge generational conflicts. When millennials were kids, they were handed participation trophies. However, people can't dish the onus on millennials. That one's all on our parents. We were also pushed to take harder AP classes in high school just so we could get into a great college. We've been told that we're great, special, and unique which has caused some millennials to feel entitled to greatness.

In a viral video, Simon Sinek outlines the four reasons why millennials are not only different, but may struggle to assimilate with the rest of society: <u>parenting, technology, impatience, and (corporate) environment</u>.

» We had 'helicopter parents' who always knew what we were up to and gave us participation trophies. We can't have whatever we want whenever we want it; that's not how the real world works. Simon cites a 2012

Harvard study, which showed that social media and phone usage activated dopamine within the human brain. He notes that drugs, gambling, and alcohol also cause a release of dopamine, which is highly addictive. He jokes that there are age restrictions on the purchase of drugs, gambling, and alcohol, but not on social media. Sinek claims that millennials are a byproduct of failed parenting strategies, which has left us without the ability to cope with our emotions.

» Instead of turning to people, millennials turn to technology to solve their stress, which just self-perpetuates the addiction and provides only temporary relief. Our inability to form deep and meaningful relationships has forced us to rely on the superficial nature of social media. We simply don't have the coping mechanisms to deal with stress, so we turn to technology because it's always there for us.

» It's no secret that millennials are impatient, and thrive on instant gratification. Sinek sites Amazon 2-day shipping, binge watching Netflix, and Tinder dates as things that have prevented us from the need to learn the social coping mechanisms to delay gratification. The reality is, job satisfaction, strength of relationships, and love, are slow, meandering, and messy processes.

» The unfortunate reality is that the corporate environments of today care more about the numbers than they do about the people. The short-term returns matter more to them than the long-term life of the human. Quarterly profits supersede the mental anguish that can stick with an employee for decades. The environment we've been accustomed to doesn't teach us that life requires balance, and that it may take time for things to materialize. The worst part of it all is that millennials blame themselves. It's the corporate world and lack of good leadership that is making millennials feel the way they do. It's the companies' responsibility to pick up the slack and build up confidence and social skills that weren't taught to millennials by their parent's decades ago.

For Simon Sinek's full interview (which I've briefly summarized above), please reference the citations below (2).

I don't want to focus on weaknesses because that's not how growth is facilitated. However, every generation, human, and business has weaknesses. No one is perfect.

Although I'm a huge proponent of strengths-based training, ignoring weaknesses is simply naïve. This generation has an instant gratification, individualistic ideology. "I want it personalized and I want it now." Is this a terrible thing? No. Ironically, this is part of our strengths as well. Millennials have high expectations, but that doesn't mean that all of those standards are realistic. Our high standards can both drive us forward, and hold us back from the progress we seek.

We all need to work together to assimilate. High standards create successful companies. We should not shy away from peak performance. What we should do is merge ideologies as time passes.

<u>What makes us weak is what makes us different, and what makes us different is what gives us strength</u>. The solution to all our problems lies within our ability to empathize with one another. Millennials with opportunity recognition skills realize that opportunities are abundant. The age of technology has provided opportunities for everyone, regardless of our age. *The Millennial Merger* is all about recognizing opportunities and leveraging each other's knowledge to create a better tomorrow. Once the generations understand each other, we can work together to develop this masterpiece we call life.

Moore's Law. (n.d.). Retrieved January 09, 2017, from http://www.mooreslaw.org/

Simon Sinek on Millennials in the Workplace. (2016, October 29). Retrieved January, 2017, from https://www.youtube.com/watch?v=hER0Qp6QJNU

■ The Victims

nevitably, in every generation there are a group of rebels who try to say how shitty their peers are. "All my peers suck."

Or, how about this one: "I was born in the wrong generation." For those who surround themselves with millennial victims, here's my little tip of advice: RUN! If you employ one of these people, it may be beneficial to let them go. Victims, pessimists, and defeatists will never help you (or your company) grow. It's in their very nature to bring those around them down. This problem is not only synonymous with millennials; every generation has these characters.

If you happen to work with one of these people, do something about it. Go speak to your superiors about the one person in the office that brings everyone down. If your boss doesn't want to do anything about it, go find a new job. Life is too short to surround yourself with people who are always playing the victim card. They bring others down to lift themselves up. I have the utmost respect for those who consistently find the good in every situation. Finding the negativity in any moment is taking the easy way out.

To generalize all millennials and say they all suck is insane. There are people in our generation that are making huge advancements in technology, healthcare, and globalization. And you have the audacity to herd those people into this "negative categorization" that you call millennials? Get a life.

Vice versa, to generalize all millennials and say we're all awesome is just as insane. There are good apples and bad apples. If you're going to play the victim card, you're just the sour apple. Get off your high horse and do something different, or at least find a group of people you can relate to.

If you're a millennial reading this and you think the rest of our generation sucks, stop. Be the solution and not the problem. Find a group of people that you like and thrive. I can't throw a pity-party for you. Playing the victim card will get you nowhere in this world.

There are two types of victims: blamers and complainers.

» Blamers – They love to put the onus on external forces. "It was the market. It was my boss. It was the weather. It was my landlord. It was my neighbor's second cousin." No – it was YOU! Take accountability for your faults and move forward. Not taking accountability for your own failures will only make you a victim of circumstance. Change your mindset and start being a creator of circumstance.

» Complainers – They love to focus on everything that's wrong with the situation and nothing that's right. These people typically tell you that they're not pessimists, they're realists. Bullshit! What you focus on, you attract. If you're going to focus on all the problems in life, what are you going to get? More problems.

If you surround yourself with these types of people, you end up becoming one. Who you hang around is who you become. Playing the victim card is a slippery slope that's easy to create and hard to break.

I caution you to keep an eye out for these people. Victims are the people who dish the blame and justify their actions based on circumstances. They aren't good at taking accountability for their actions, and most of all, life always seems to happen to them, not for them. <u>They play victim to situations and find the shadow in every light</u>.

Everyone has someone in their life that's just a hassle to deal with. I'm not trying to be a pessimist, but out of all your relationships, there are one or two that emotionally drain you. Cut the fat and surround yourself with people that make you the best version of you.

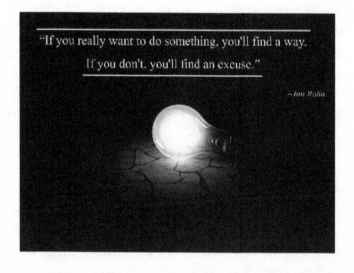

■ The Bad Apples

Millennials often get a bad rap. Entitled. Self-centered. Egotistical. Lazy. We've heard it all. The reality is that every generation has a group of bad apples. Mobsters? Druggies? Con-artists? Don't be so quick to point the finger.

There's no such thing as the perfect generation. Everyone has their weaknesses. Most of our flaws are structured around our formative years. The technology boom. The housing bubble. Terrorism. Shifting global economies. Safe spaces. We're a product of our environments.

Every generation goes through a stage where they are young, defiant and different. That's part of the evolutionary process. They said the same thing about Generation X, 20 years before us. As millennials, we're always looking for ways to be different and stand out, both from a generational standpoint and a peer-to-peer standpoint. This need to stand out has caused mass production and consumption of social media (both from individuals and corporations).

Is there a serious social media addiction issue in this country (and around the world)? Without a doubt, but it's not confined to one generation. It's rampant across society.

Although the social movement has caused some negative stereotypes, realize that this social media addiction has done good for our generation as well. Millennials happen to be extremely outspoken about issues across the world. Apologize for having an opinion? I don't think so. How about, "Respect the fact that I have a backbone and the ability to form my own beliefs."

Just like Isaac Newton said, "For every action there is an equal and opposite reaction."

Are you one of those people complaining about how millennials are always listening to loud "techno" music? Go create or invest in a hearing aid company. It's a sure win in the future.

Complaining about how millennials are always looking down at their phones and don't know how to communicate face-to-face? Start a consulting practice teaching younger generations how to properly communicate and engage in a multi-generational workplace. I have a head start on that one!

Look, in any situation you can focus on one of two things. You can either complain about the problem or come up with a solution. You can either move toward the darkness or toward the light. While you nitpick this generation, there's someone out there making money off our inadequacies. You can complain about all the terrible things millennials do, or you can engage them in a way that will bring out the best version of themselves.

There's a structural crisis in America and it's not the millennials' fault; it's the world's fault. It's easy to dish the blame for society's problems on millennials because we're different. Being different is what every generation aspires to be. Generations should not be looking at millennials as a zero-sum game, everyone can win. Life is about creating something magical so that the generations after you have it a little better, easier, brighter than you did. Our role in society is to pave the road for those who come after us. If you'd like to argue that point, look at what your parents tried to do for you.

Maybe the problem here is that we're simply mixing up the story of "bad apples" with "different apples."

■ The New American Dream

I t's interesting to watch the evolution of "The American Dream" over the years. It's a coveted plateau that many across the world yearn for. So, what is the new American dream? It depends who you are. What's your American dream?

I would caution you to not define "The Dream" based on cultural constructs that have been a part of our society for centuries. Millennials look at the dream a lot differently than previous generations.

The old American dream looked something like this: buy a house and raise a family. Sounds pretty basic, right? My mom told me that when she was 23, she bought her first house. I thought that was insane! Why would you go lock yourself down at 23 years old? You have your whole life to do that. But at the time, that was the thing to do.

The "New American Dream" has more so to do with experiences from our early years: <u>live debt free and experience what the world has to offer</u>. Because we're the most educated generation (in the most formal sense of the word), we have more student loan debt than any of our predecessors. For the first time in history, student loan debt outweighs credit card debt (1).

The reason we want to "experience what the world has to offer" is because items are just that: items! To a millennial, things don't make us happy; experiences do. Seventy-three percent of millennials said that "being happy" is what makes you successful, whereas 36% said "being rich" is what makes you successful (2). There's a paradigm shift in thinking.

Here's the psychology behind it: "If I'm going to work for 40 years, I'm going to have a great time doing it! Whether it's here, there, or in China, I'm going to enjoy something that I spend most my life doing. If your company or product doesn't make me happy, I'm going to go find a company or product that will!" The trick is for employers, salespeople, marketers and organizations alike to create engaging experiences. Business is pleasure and pleasure is business. If it's not, go find a place to work where business is pleasurable. You won't regret it.

Please do not be mistaken when I'm talking about engaging experiences. It includes both your customers and your employees. In today's age, your customers are your employees and your employees are your customers. If you create a great experience for your employees, would you say it's translated to your customers? Of course, and vice versa. If you create a great experience for your customers, that's translated to your employees.

In modern society, companies need to look to create brand evangelists. Companies like Apple and Nike don't ask customers to share their experiences. Yet the customers still do. Why? They love the company or product so much that they feel it's their responsibility and obligation to share their experience with the world. If you create magical experiences for people, the rewards will come back tenfold.

The old American Dream was to work hard your whole life so that you have enough money to retire nicely. The new way? The journey is the destination, so enjoy the ride. Is it the fact that "Millennials can't take pain"? Maybe for some. It's more so the fact that if you're not creating an "enjoyable experience" in the workplace, employees will go someplace else that will satisfy that need.

It used to be that employees choose a job and that's what they stuck with for 40 years. They retired, received a nice watch, a pension, and then waited for the clock to run out. If you made a hasty decision 40 years back, you were stuck. It was frowned upon to leave your job for a different opportunity.

Today people are leaving their jobs all the time. "If I'm not happy, peace out!" There are thousands of companies out there that can make me happy. Why would I stick with yours? It's a different way of thinking.

My hypothesis is that people in society went from "having a job" to "fulfilling a purpose." People went from "managing all life's responsibilities" to "designing a lifestyle." If you're not waking up on a Monday morning excited to tackle the week, you're in the wrong job. Go find your purpose or your own version of "The American Dream."

When people ask me what I do, there are too many responses. There are too many opportunities and actions to accurately describe what I really do. So, my response has simply changed to "livin' the dream." I decided to make a commitment to be happy, and that's what has made me successful. I suggest you do the same. That's the "New" American Dream.

Jasthi, S. (n.d.). Credit Card, Student Loans and Mortgage Debt in the U.S. Retrieved January, 2017, from https://www.nerdwallet.com/blog/credit-card-data/credit-card-student-loans-mortgage-debt-comparison/

Attracting and Retaining Millennials in the Global Workplace. (2016, June 24). Retrieved January, 2017, from http://www.aperianglobal.com/attracting-retaining-millennials-global-workplace/

■ Commitment

Millennials are committed to change. The question is, are you committed to meeting them half way?

We don't get what we want in life, we don't get what we expect, and we certainly don't get what we deserve. We only get what we're 100% committed to.

Everything worth attaining in life takes a commitment. Not an 85% commitment. Not a 95% commitment. A 100% commitment. The true rock star pushes it to 110% and above. If you want something in life, you must go all in. Going all in requires some sacrifice.

Everyone who has gotten to this point of the book needs to make some decisions about which concepts they're going to implement, and which concepts they're going to move to the side. As I spoke about at the beginning of this experience, most people will not align with all the concepts throughout the book. That's okay.

Millennials are committed to a few things:

» Making the world a better place.

» Enjoying the work experience.

» Working with people they like.

» Working for a cause they believe in.

» Experiencing all the pleasures earth has to offer.

When leaders and followers are committed to the same goal, the stars become aligned. There is a sense of congruency in the team's actions and all the energy is flowing in one direction. The millennials are committed to making global change. The question is, are you committed to working with them?

Change is a choice. When you make a choice, you commit to one decision and put all the others behind you. We're not committed when our thoughts are moving forward, but our actions are left behind. Commitment means your thoughts, emotions and body are all driven in the same direction. True commitment takes congruent action.

To commit takes discipline, there's no way around it. Just like Jim Collins spoke about in his book *Good to Great*, the three aspects of every successful business include:

» Disciplined people

» Disciplined thought

» Disciplined action

Discipline takes focus, and focus comes naturally when we have a sense of <u>awareness</u>. Awareness is the first step to gaining momentum. It may take some discipline, but over time awareness will become part of who you are; not just what you do.

Everyone needs to make the choice to commit to the changes they want to see within their lives. We all have an internal code – an internal law that we follow both consciously and subconsciously. Our guiding principles are what shape our commitments and actions throughout our own lives. It's a personal ideology that should be ever evolving for individuals as they move throughout their lives.

» Commit to your vision for a better tomorrow, both for your life and the world around you.

» Commit to constantly adapting your empowering belief systems and letting go of your limitations.

» Commit to being guided by your own internal code that you've developed over time.

» Commit to the top five things on your bucket list; the things you want to experience before you pass.

» Commit to your success rituals, and forgoing the habits that are getting in the way of attaining what you want.

» Commit to being accountable for both your successes and failures throughout life.

» Commit to the future you see, not the future others see for you.

To get what you want in the future, you must be willing to work today for a better tomorrow. Commitment is a choice and everyone has the personal power of decision, whether they realize it or not. Many people allow others to make commitments and decisions on their behalf. Giving up your personal power is also a choice, one that most people make unconsciously.

Every day we wake up, we make a choice. A choice to live exactly as we did yesterday, or to change and take our lives in the direction we want to go.

Your commitment to the changes you make should be based on the vision you have for your future. I know commitment can be intimidating and scary at times. Just like we spoke about before, commitment starts with awareness. Once you're self-aware, you can put all your energy into the first step. That's how we start to create that magical momentum in our lives.

It doesn't matter what you've done. It doesn't matter what you know. It doesn't matter what you think you're qualified or unqualified to do. The only thing that matters is what you choose to commit to today.

The only thing in life you have to commit to is the next step. That's it. Don't overcomplicate it. Don't under complicate it. Just take the next step. It's probably a lot easier than you're making it seem. Your health, your career, your relationships, your finances, your spirituality, your fun, your attitude – these are all things you can decide to change and improve over time.

When I'm doing workshops with corporations, I hear the same thing over and over: "I want to become a millionaire" or "I want to make more money. How do I do that?"

Everyone wants to make more money and that's great, but no one can do it for you. Your journey to wealth has to start with your commitment to improvement. Most motivational speakers get up on stage, pump you up and make you feel good. Then, 24 hours later, it's back to the same old shit.

Listening to a speaker, thought leader, or coach is a waste of time if you don't commit to "take action." I'm not talking about massive action. I'm talking about the first step.

If you commit to the first step right now, then this book was worth the time. If you decide to put this book down and don't commit to any new actions, ask yourself, "Why?"

Commit to working with millennials. Commit to improving your personal and professional life. And, commit to living the life you've always dreamed of.

■ Conclusion

The **Millennial Merger** was meant to be written as a meeting of the minds. This was by no means a ploy to prove millennials as an all superior race. We need to make sure we don't fall into stereotypical traps that divide this generation.

This piece was meant to bring to light some of our strengths and weaknesses based on our nature and nurture.

I would like to take this opportunity to personally thank all the generations that came before us. On behalf of all millennials, I say, *Thank you.* The generations before us created TVs, airplanes, smartphones, the Internet, sliced bread, and have dramatically increased the quality of life as we know it. There aren't enough words in the English language that I could use to express my gratitude.

I know with every ounce of certainty in my body that the millennial generation will take the baton you've handed us and run forward. We'll make strides in technology, medicine, politics, and globalization that this world has never seen before. As we attain more influence within society, it's important that we utilize our power for improving the world around us. Just like you did for us, we must make sure we provide a better life for those who will come after us.

Although many of the big organizations put us in the precarious situations we face today, they're also the ones who are best positioned to help turn things around. One day, not so far from now, millennials will be running both the public and private sector. Our generation has leaders who can positively impact people across the globe. This is part of the reason why bridging the generational gap is so important!

The future I see for this generation looks a lot different from where we're at as a society today. Today, we're 1,000 steps away (maybe even more). This book was meant to be step number one.

All I want to do is start a conversation. My only job here was to create a spark, because sparks lead to fires. With enough oxygen (people), a fire can turn into a movement. Movements happen through momentum and momentum can change the world. Now that I've taken the first step, what I need you to do is take the second.

This is the first iteration of the millennial ideology, and I expect it to change, grow and evolve as a way of thinking over time. Great leaders are always looking for constructive criticism and feedback. I'm looking for you to reach out to me via email or social media and voice your opinion on this growing ideology.

I know you didn't agree with every concept in this book, and I'm glad you didn't. I purposefully put some polarizing philosophies in here because I know that in today's world, the only things that get noticed are outside the realm of ordinary.

I'm looking to discover other ideologies to help facilitate the adoption of *The Millennial Merger* to the rest of society. Future generations will read this book to help assimilate to the constructs we hold closest to our hearts. *The Millennial Merger* will be a continuing conversation about an evolving philosophy to create positive change in the 21st century.

Naturally, there are many millennials who don't identify with some of these concepts. They have this contrarian viewpoint on life and they despise everything the millennial generation stands for. I'm so happy that I get to identify with those people because they stand for something. Standing for something is 1,000 times better than standing for nothing.

You can complain about how this generation stinks or you can go be the change you want to see in the world. One of our core constructs as millennials is individualism, and by going against the grain, you're directly aligning with the construct that defines us.

As you move on with your life, I need you to realize that there is a ton of messed up crap in our world. There are divides in society politically, religiously, racially, financially, and in every other conceivable way. Every day we fight the battle between accepting what is and changing the world to what could *be.*

In a divided world, the answer is always love and abundance. My success doesn't come at the cost of your success. Success is a choice, and success is abundant. I think many people in this world have fallen into the trap of zero-sum outcomes. This world is going to continue to experience unrest. It's those that bring light to darkness that will free our society from the fear and anguish we will inevitably continue to experience.

But, if no one else is willing to be the change when the world's shit hits the fan. Don't worry, I'll be there. I just hope you'll join me on that journey.

■ 15 Millennial Tips

Writing this book has been a personal emotional rollercoaster. I really hope you'll reach out to me and give some feedback, but first, I have a few tips for some of the millennials reading. There are things that we can do as a generation to ease this meeting-of-the-minds process. It's our duty to facilitate this merger, just like it is for the generations that come before and after us. So here we go!

1. Don't quit your job just because you went from happy to content. See if there's anything you can do to make yourself happy again. Life is a journey, full of ups, downs, lefts and rights. It won't always go your way. Learn how to adapt, change and move forward with the hand you're dealt. It's a skill you'll be thankful for down the road. If you're a little uncomfortable, you're probably heading in the right direction. Always remember, the journey is the destination. As Buddha said, "<u>At the end of the way is freedom. Till then, patience</u>."

2. Please don't assume that you are the most fascinating person in the room. I frequently tell people, "If you're the smartest (or most fascinating) person in the room, you're in the wrong room." I hope that's not the first time you've heard that saying! Thinking you're the best thing since sliced bread is feeding into the negative stereotype of egotism, self-centeredness, and other adjectives people equate with millennials. Walk into a room and look to help people. As we've discussed, the

more people you help, the more often you'll become "the most fascinating person in the room." If you're walking through every doorway thinking about yourself, you've lost the battle. If you're thinking about "we," you're on the right track.

3. Let go of the shit that's holding you back. We all have childhood dreams and we all have childhood nightmares. Some of your dreams may come to fruition down the road, but some of them you should probably let go of. Some of your childhood nightmares will also come to fruition, but only if you keep focusing on them. A sense of nostalgia will only keep you in the past. Am I saying it's not good to ponder on the good olé days? Hell no. Crack open a beer, kick it with your friends, and reminisce on the good times. However, when you wake up the next morning, it's time to ride the wave toward the future. If you keep living in the past and complaining about how "life will never be how it used to," you'll be stuck in a never-ending rut of reminiscence.

4. Be(come) interested in other people. There's nothing worse than talking to someone who is only looking to talk about themselves. Don't start a conversation just to talk about yourself. If you're going to your friends, family, significant others and other relationships to "get" instead of "give," you're never going to be truly happy. <u>Quality relationships are the key to a happy life</u> (1). To have quality relationships, you have to be interested in other people.

5. As we grow and mature, we will have more responsibility on our shoulders. In the coming years, we're not just providing for ourselves, we're providing for our kids, our parents and our society. It's our responsibility to make this world a better place and tap into our potential while doing so. In order to be the true segue from the good ole days to the age of technology, we need to completely unleash from our limitations; and our

limitations are all the old beliefs in our lives (and society) that no longer help us today. We need to decide what beliefs will drive us forward now.

6. Face-to-face interactions are becoming increasingly important in a world that's becoming more technologically advanced. It's time to realize that we must learn and hone our social skills so that we can pass it on to our kids. If we don't do this, the art of face-to-face communication will literally die. As much as technology has bridged the communication gap, there's nothing on this planet that will ever replace face-to-face interactions. I know there are millennials who struggle with this skill set. It's important that we're conscientious of this inadequacy moving forward. We can't be the generation that let face-to-face interactions die.

7. We need to stay away from the blame-game, because blaming someone never changed an outcome. Don't blame the big banks, don't blame your mom, don't blame the baby boomers, don't blame your employer, your landlord, the economy, the Apple store, the media, the airlines, the weatherman, the Pokémon, or anything else for that matter. The only person responsible for your success or failure is you. Will there be people who help you along the way? Absolutely, but don't sit there waiting for the opportunity, and then blame circumstance when it doesn't knock on your door. If you can't find a door, go build one. Once you build it, knock that bitch down and seize the opportunity.

8. Get outside your comfort zone. Many millennials love to stay comfortable because it's all they know. It's easy to stay on your phone all day and get lost in the digital world. It's easy to stay at a job you hate just because you're overpaid. It's comfortable because it's something you're familiar with and have control over. However, no one ever became successful by staying comfortable. Put your phone down and get out in the

world. You may discover something that could change your life.

9. Be a person of your word. At the end of the day, real respect is earned, not given. Don't just expect to get respect because you're a millennial. You're making us look bad! Check your ego at the door and do what you say you're going to do. There's nothing worse than working with someone who is all talk.

10. Older people are trees of knowledge. Their trunks are thicker. They have more branches; they've been through more seasons. Ask them questions. Pick their brains. Fish for insight. The quickest way to gain respect from an elder is to show them that you're conscious of their experience. Although the world is forever changing, our elders are the ones who have lived the change. I promise, some extra insight won't hurt you.

11. Pay off your debt. Don't wait for Uncle Sam to bail you out. Our country has too many other problems. If you're waiting for that day, it may never come. The best thing my grandma ever taught me was to only spend the money that I have. If you're looking to invest your money, the safest investment in any economy is an investment in yourself. Invest in your personal education, knowledge, and experiences. No one can ever take it from you.

12. Familiarize yourself with the Dunning-Kruger Effect. Here is Wikipedia's description: "The Dunning–Kruger effect is a cognitive bias in which relatively unskilled individuals suffer from illusory superiority, mistakenly assessing their ability to be much higher than it really is." Basically, the stupider you are, the more you think you know. Smart people know what they don't know. This tends to be why stupid people beat their chest, while the smart ones keep to themselves. When in doubt, asking better questions will give you better answers. Thinking that you know everything is just

proving that you know nothing. Learning is a lifetime sport for everyone. Start training for it.

13. Be the light when there is darkness. Show confidence when there is fear. People want someone to look up to. If you're constantly helping others, you'll eventually find what it is you're looking for. I tell all my friends, "Success is only one handshake away." The best way to make that handshake count is by smiling. When everything is going to shit in your world, just smile. No one smiles anymore. Smiles are infectious and can literally change your life. It's the first thing I do when I wake up and when I go to sleep. There's no such thing as waking up on the wrong side of the bed. Make the choice, put on a smile and seize the day.

14. Seek the opinions of others. We are a very opinionated generation. Again, it's both the problem and the solution. We don't like to agree with everyone, just for the sake of being likable. If you have an opinion, it's okay to befriend someone with an opposing view. You're not going to die if you hear from the other side of the table. This is how people build that little skill called empathy. Walk a day in someone else's shoes. Eat their food and drink their Kool Aid. Just make sure you don't start preaching your beliefs. No one wants your ideas shoved down their throat.

15. Be irreplaceable. If you don't love what you're doing, start searching for something that makes you exceptional. When I was working for Tony, my customers would come up to me and tell me that "I could be the next Tony Robbins." I'm not the next Tony Robbins. I'm not the next Steve Jobs. I'm not the next Mark Zuckerberg. I'm the first Jesse Henry. No one can replace me and no one can compete with me because I'm in a category of my own. Everyone should adopt this type of ideology. You are the one and only you. No one can replace you. No one can be you, and no one can make decisions for you. You are

special and unlike anyone else on this planet. Being unique is living your own special type of awesome.

Waldinger, R. (2015, November). What makes a good life? Lessons from the longest study on happiness. Retrieved January, 2017, from http://www.ted.com/talks/robert_waldinger_what_ma kes_a_good_life_lessons_from_the_longest_study_on_hap piness_language=en

Quadailty

I must admit, I had no intentions of putting these last two sections in this book. There's little to no tie in to Millennial's, as these next two concepts apply to every entity (both businesses and humans alike). You will not find citations or quotes in these sections because this is my own research based on experiences from my own life. The only place you will find out more information on these concepts is on my site, www.Quadality.com.

There's fear, there's embarrassment, and there's a ton of pain surrounding how these concepts were 'stumbled upon.' I'll leave the story of *how* I came up with these concepts for another day (or another book). The concepts are still extremely rough, and part of my hesitation on including these constructs in the book was that I don't "have it all figured out yet." But, let's be honest, do we ever really have it all figured out? Never.

Since finishing up this book, I've taken on a new philosophical perspective; one where my reality is no better or worse than anyone else's. But, there's no denying that my reality is different than the 7 billion other realities on planet earth. For those who question the multiverse theory (the hypothetical set of possible universes) you need only look in a place with 50 or so other people. You may notice that you're in the presence of 50 different realities, who all happen to be coexisting in the same place at the same time. As you move on in life, your reality will be separated from those 50 people –

they will continue to live in their reality just as you will in yours. This has led me to believe that "reality" is a very fluid term based on time, space, matter, energy, and the objective and subjective nature of our circumstances.

Quite simply, the concept of "Quadality" came about from questioning the nature of reality. This has been the timeless question that's plagued philosophers for millennia. So, before we tackle Quadality, let's tackle the question "what is the nature of reality?"

A simple Google search gives 2 definitions for the word "reality"

» the world or the state of things as they actually exist, as opposed to an idealistic or notional idea of them.

» the state or quality of having existence or substance. These are both fairly straightforward definitions of reality.

One could interpret these definitions as holding a sense of objectivity.

But, this brings up the other age old philosophical question "Is reality subjective or objective?" And the answer I've come up with is *both.* If we remove our objective reality, our subjective reality ceases to exist. And vis versa, if we remove our subjective reality, then our objective reality ceases to exist.

We need the objective reality to form our subjective reality. And, we need our subjective reality in order to perceive (or sense) the objective world. Both subjective and objective world exist simultaneously. We cannot remove one from the other.

So, if the objective nature of reality is the "physical" reality that we perceive on a daily basis; it begs the question, "what is the subjective nature of reality?"

The subjective nature of reality is mental, emotional, and spiritual. It's <u>completely unique to the individual,</u>

and holds very little (or no) objective reality. But, this doesn't make the subjective reality any less real to the individual who's perceiving it.

This is the basis for the concept of "Quadality."

Quadality describes the nature of our mental, physical, emotional, and spiritual realities existing simultaneously and equilaterally. This "4-dimensional" version of reality exists within us individually at ALL times. We experience these 4 dimensions simultaneously, yet have the ability to isolate each of the dimensions for assessment and optimization purposes. Since our subjective and objective worlds coexist, we do not actually live in reality; we live in our own mental, physical, emotional, and spiritual versions of reality. Hence the term "Quadality." This has formed the belief that we do not live in "Reality," we live in "Quadality." This can simply be thought of as '4-dimensional reality.'

The basis of Quadality currently stands on 3 major (scientific) concepts.

1. Quantum Computing – Instead of 1 OR 0, Quantum computing allows states to render both 1's AND 0's at the same time. Particles having the ability to be in multiple positions simultaneously is referred to as quantum superposition. Allowing for 2 states to exist simultaneously has lead us to many hypothesis. We don't live in a subjective or objective world – we live in both (they exist simultaneously). This entanglement of realities exists in a quantum state. This means our reality (or Quadality) is quantum in nature.

2. Modalities – These are the lenses through which we view the world. We typically view the world through our senses – (visual, auditory, kinesthetic, olfactory, and gustatory are the basics). But, believers in Quadality tend to believe that our senses do not stop at our physical extremities. Sense of balance, pain, temperature,

homeostasis, and emotion are all things we sense with our brain, they just don't happen to have an opposing physical appendage for external perception. These senses could be construed as subjective; whereas sights, smells, and sounds could be viewed as more objective modalities.

3. Dualities (Specifically Wave-Particle Duality) – Explains that all particles can be described in terms of both particles and waves. Both (particle and wave) states exist simultaneously within all of the most elementary particles on the planet. Humans have a physical (or particle) nature, but we also give off electromagnetic waves concurrently. On the other hand, when Einstein was studying the photoelectric effect, he noticed that when UV light (waves) hit a surface, it emitted electrons (particles). Wave-Particle Duality coincides with quantum mechanics, and proves to humans that multiple states can exist simultaneously.

Here is a visual representation of how we can think about "Quadality"

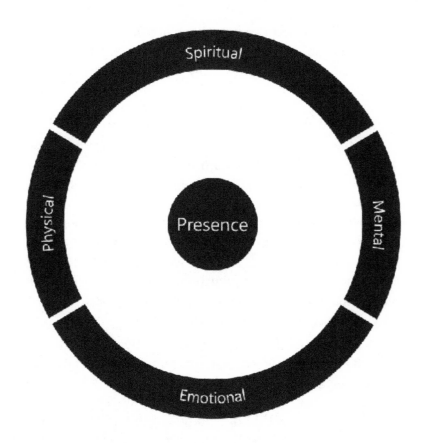

All ontological models should include presence in the middle because we cannot remove ourselves from our presence. We can reach outside of our current reality, but we cannot physically remove ourselves from the time, space, and matter in which we currently exist.

If Quadality describes the nature of our mental, physical, emotional, and spiritual realities existing simultaneously, naturally, we must develop clear definitions for these constructs.

Of course, there is a subjective nature to the definitions of these 4 constructs, and each of us will determine these definitions based on our own nature and nurture. These 4 states have been studied for thousands of years, so the internet can provide you with alternative narratives describing the nature of these states.

Defining Mental, Physical, Emotional, and Spiritual:

» **Mental Reality** – Describes the processes going on inside of our head. Our mind is the greatest tool we've been given. We can achieve expanded awareness, recall past experiences, and will ourselves away from pain and toward pleasure with just our mind. Humans experience thought patterns that occur time and time again; and our mind is the only matter with the capability of continuing these patterns, or changing them for a more desirable outcome. Our mental reality exists equilaterally to our physical, emotional, and spiritual reality.

» **Physical Reality** – Describes our physiology (body), and the material world that surrounds us. Our physical reality exists at the intersection of time, space, and matter. It's deeply affected by the 11 systems that are always running within our body. Overall, it's our inputs (exercise, nutrition, rest) that ultimately affects how our bodily systems run, and therefore effects our physical reality. Our external environment impacts how our body responds to situations on a moment to moment basis. Our physical reality exists equilaterally to our mental, emotional, and spiritual reality.

» **Emotional Reality** – Describes our interpretations (and beliefs) about our other realities. Humans have the ability to attach meaning (and labels) to situations; and these meanings dictate our emotional state and wellbeing at any given moment. Emotion, quite literally, means "energy in motion." All our desires are based on the emotional states (or the energy) that we seek. Without emotion (and spirituality) we're nothing more than a computer with inputs and outputs. Emotions take our mental, subjective world, and turns them to conscious expressions, which in turn change our physical reality. Our emotions determine how we express ourselves, how we communicate, and how we set expectations for both ourselves and others. Our emotional reality exists equilaterally to our mental, physical, and spiritual reality.

» **Spiritual Reality** – Describes our connection to other forms of energy. Despite the common misconception, one does not need to be religious in order to be spiritual. Connecting with other sentient beings and accessing information from the collective consciousness gives us a sense of connection and fulfillment. <u>One may think of spirituality as the transfer of energy</u>. Communication, food, animals, architecture, nature, ethics – these things that we take for granted are the foundation of human sentience and connection. If our ancestors did something, then that something retains a certain spiritual counterpart to it (as it is a part of our collective history). The collective consciousness provides the foundation (or substructure) for our society to thrive upon. All innovation would be impossible without connection to the past (or the collective consciousness). The discovery of expanded states of consciousness like centeredness, acceptance, transcendence, and connection help us to attain spiritual enlightenment. Spirituality is about *connection* – and happens on a day to day basis whether we recognize it or not. Our spiritual reality exists equilaterally to our mental, physical, and emotional reality.

Here's how it breaks down:

» Physical expressions hold mental, emotional, and spiritual counterparts.

» Mental expressions hold physical, emotional, and spiritual counterparts.

» Emotional expressions hold physical, mental, and spiritual counterparts.

» Spiritual expressions hold physical, emotional, and mental counterparts.

I know this because my physical reality fell apart, and very quickly I started to notice my mental, emotional, and spiritual reality follow suit. Up until recently I had not considered myself a spiritual individual because I couldn't "imagine some guy with a beard and a toga up in the sky." Although that's an oversimplification of how many think about spirituality (or religion), I needed to go through tough times to understand that the definitions of mental, physical, emotional, and spiritual are not created by society; they're created within. Once we remove the social constructs of what "spiritual" means to others, we can come up with our own definition that best suits our reality as we see it.

These 4 realities cannot be turned off because of their simultaneous existence. We can ignore aspects of our reality, but that doesn't remove their individual (and simultaneous) existence from our lives.

In general, our Quadality (or simultaneous realities) exist in 2 very distinct states:

1. Alignment – all 4 realities are creating aligned thoughts, feelings, and actions. This is when we feel 'guided' to do things via purposeful action and intuitive sentience. We feel pulled into action, and peak performance seems effortless. This is our *flow* state.

2. Misalignment – one of our realities may be causing an asymmetrical perspective. This is when emotional blocks and inner conflicts start eating away at our psyche. We must hone our ability to recognize honestly and sincerely that there is *friction* in our lives. Once we

identify the friction, we can experience exponential momentum because of our unwavering faith toward becoming aligned and congruent.

It's no secret which of these is preferred. The conscious alignment of all 4 simultaneous realities is a constant and never ending journey. But, just when we think we "have it all figured out" – life throws another curve ball in our way to throw us out of alignment. It's our ability to recognize the misalignment, come to terms with it, and actively pursue our newfound version of enlightenment that makes our lives unique and purposeful.

Our mental, physical, emotional, and spiritual wellbeing has been studied for millennia. Quadality is nothing "revolutionary" per-say; it's simply a culmination of the collective consciousness. Quadality (as a philosophy) will continue to explore research and historical data to further develop the ideology as a whole.

As I mentioned before, this is a work in progress. But, I felt it was necessary to share this perspective with you because I've been through times of unbearable amounts of friction in my life. And, it wasn't until I realized that I was living multiple realities simultaneously that I had the ability to discern which area I needed to work on to make all the other realities fall into alignment.

This perspective deepened my understanding of who I am as an individual. <u>We can only understand others from our own level of consciousness</u>, and vis versa, <u>we can only discover others as deeply as they've discovered themselves</u>. If we want to further discover internal and external realities, we must create ideologies that allow us to transcend conventional wisdom to better understand ourselves.

This is why Quadality can become foundational on your journey to seek a higher level of understanding of reality, and why I've shared it with you today. If our consciousness creates our reality, then, if we want to change our reality, we must change our consciousness.

■ The 9 Energy Gaps

One of the largest epiphanies someone can have is when they realize that life all comes down to learning how to *manipulate energy.* And, every coach, consultant, therapist, counselor or mentor is trying to help you do one thing – bridge the gap. Energy Gaps exist everywhere, and I've spent a lot of time trying to break them down.

In a macro sense, the gap is the space between where you are, and were you want to go (or should currently be). There will always be gaps in our lives; we can either use them to drive us forward, or hold us back.

I'm lead to believe that there are only so many potential gaps that someone can experience. So, if gaps are consistent in nature, then there must be an overarching construct that helps us systematically identify these gaps. As I started to ponder this concept – I thought deeply about my TEDx experience, my time working with Tony Robbins, and primary colors.

I know primary colors was not the concept you were expecting, but if a tripartite (3 part) construct could be used to explain one of the most complex concepts (all the colors perceivable to the human eye), then it could be used to define the gaps in our lives. Here is an image of the 3 primary gaps (inner ring), and the 6 secondary gaps (outer ring). Let me explain how they work, and how they're all interconnected.

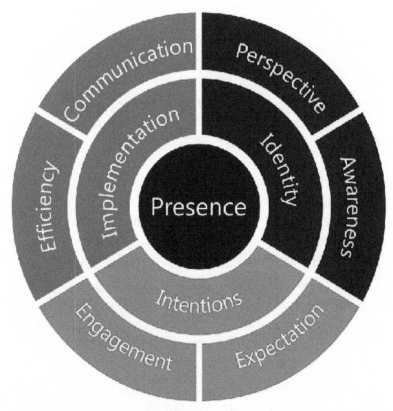

Primary Gap #1 – The Identity Gap

Our identity GAP is the distance between who we are – and who we think we *should be.* Our identity is our nature, nurture, and millions of years of evolution wrapped up into the fleeting moment. Our identity comes down to how we define ourselves.

When I say identity, I don't mean your name. Your name is just a linguistic representation of who you actually are. Your identity is the person you see in the mirror. Everyone else can see from their perspective who you are, but you're the only one who truly knows your identity at its core.

How you define yourself will determine how others will define you. "I am..." are the two most powerful words in the world – and have the ability to change *any* circumstance.

If you don't consciously create your identity you may fall into the trap of letting others define it for you. Our identity gap can be split into 2 secondary gaps:

» **The Perspective Gap** – This gap exists on a scale from (Objective Perspective to Subjective Perspective). Our objective and subjective worlds exist simultaneously. This gap is supposed to give a level of discernment to what "is how it is," as opposed to, "is how we see it." It is a culmination of our nature and nurture, and provides the lens through which we *internalize* and interpret "reality." Our perspective is based upon what's been communicated to us, and how we <u>communicate</u> to others.

» **The Awareness Gap** – This gap exists on a scale from (Internal Awareness to External Awareness). Our awareness beyond (external) is useless unless we have awareness within (internal). We are constantly becoming more aware of activity beyond and within as our sensory acuity grows from mindfulness. Our ability to consistently *externalize* both internal and external awareness will define our ability to live freely and fully. Our awareness is based on the <u>perspective</u> we utilize on a consistent basis.

Primary Gap #2 – The Intentions Gap

Our intentions gap is the distance between what we want – and what will serve our highest good (and the highest good of all). Although not all people set their intentions based on the highest good of all, those who do tend to live in a consistent state of identity alignment.

Setting our intentions *only* on self-serving outcomes will result in a lack of fulfillment. This is why we ask ourselves, "What will serve my highest good, and the highest good of all?" We want to avoid the disconnect (or gap) between what serves us, and what serves humanity as a whole. This prevents us from entering states of pity and isolation.

Aligning our personal interests, with humanities interests, is a recipe for both success and fulfillment. Humans are designed to work together, and by aligning our intentions with others, we can create mass movements.

We must seek to align our identity (who we are) with our intentions (what we want). It's not just about attaining an outcome, it's about becoming the type of person who can fulfill our wildest dreams. Our intentions gap can be split into 2 secondary gaps:

» **The Expectation Gap** – This gap exists on a scale from (Positive Energy to Negative Energy). We label things as positive or negative based on the meaning we give it. The guidelines we set for ourselves create a specification of what is good and what is bad. Shakespeare famously said, "there is nothing either good or bad, but thinking makes it so." Conflicts can arise by not accepting that standards are individualized, and expectations are going to vary based on the individual. People tend to do best when they communicate often with those who have similar expectations. Our expectations are *internalized* dialogues we have with ourselves to determine how we think the world should be, and how we will react to outcomes that align (or misalign) with our standards. Our expectations are based on our awareness at the current point in time.

» **The Engagement Gap** – This gap exists on a scale from (Highly Engaged to Highly Disengaged). The amount of action we take determines our level of engagement. Our ability to properly *externalize* and focus our energy will help us maintain desirable states of engagement. This is the gap that most managers cite as being the crux of all their problems within the organization. With a proper level of engagement, any goal is attainable. Most people tend to either over engage or under engage – but optimal engagement is an activity that takes time, awareness, and the proper expectations. Our level of engagement is based off the expectations we set for ourselves (and others) while we're in action.

Primary Gap #3 – The Implementation Gap

Our implementation gap is the distance between what we did – and what we should have done.

Most frequently, all we should have done is acted in a way that best aligned with our identity and intentions. (The 2 other primary gaps we spoke about).

Our ability to implement is what determines our ability to attain growth, happiness, success, or any other desirable emotion.

But, our lack of implementation brings about negative emotional states that start to alter our identity. We've ALL experienced poor implementation (and seen its impact on our lives).

Our implementation gap is what holds us back from getting what we want. Close this gap and watch everything you've ever wanted come to fruition. Our implementation gap can be split into 2 secondary gaps:

» **The Efficiency Gap** – This gap exists on a scale from (Highly Efficient to Highly Inefficient). Efficiency is how we gauge performance on a personal and professional level. The only way we can discover opportunities for improvement is by *internalizing* operational inefficiencies. Without a measurement of efficiency, we would have no relative means to achieve growth. This activity assesses the outcome of the <u>engagement</u>.

» **The Communication Gap** – This gap exists on a scale from (Internal Communication to External Communication). Our ability to <u>communicate</u> inefficiencies is what allows us to shift our <u>perspective</u> (which allows us to put our <u>awareness</u> on opportunities for improvement). We can then align our <u>expectations</u> with our level of <u>engagement</u> so that we can further mitigate the <u>inefficiency</u> that was initially experienced. This gives us the opportunity to better <u>communicate</u> our sentiments to further develop our <u>perspective</u>. The circle keeps going around and around (look at the picture of the 9 Energy Gaps to further internalize this paragraph)! Communication allows us to **externalize** our thoughts, emotions, and actions. Communication is what allows us to grow our perspective over time.

Gaps have a fluid nature to them. An identity gap could have tons of different uses depending on the situation it's applied to. If you've watched my <u>TEDx Talk</u> (The Theory of Success), then you'll be able to see the direct correlation between the 3 Primary Gaps, and the 3 pillars of that TEDx Talk (which were perspective, strategy, and execution). The 3 Gaps, and the 3 pillars, help people identify <u>who they are, what they want</u>, and <u>what they're going to do about it</u>.

As you may have suspected – the concept of Quadality, and the 9 Energy Gaps, are interconnected. Explaining their interconnectedness is not simple, and even further deviates from the topic of millennials. As Einstein once famously said, "if you can't explain it simply, you don't understand it well enough."

I will save the explanation for the next book and the next adventure. Until then, I will push to further develop my understanding of myself, and the world around me. It is through that lens that I can transcend conventional wisdom, and create an abundance of resources for humanity to thrive upon.

Until Next Time...

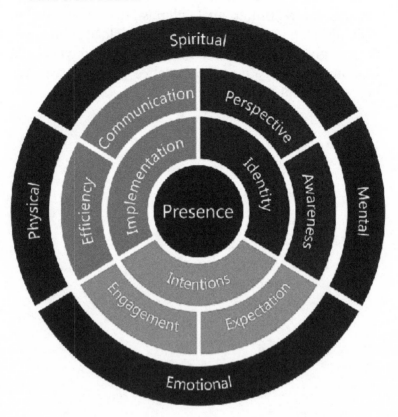

With love, gratitude, and abundance,

-JH

Jesse Henry

■ About the Author

Jesse Henry is on a journey to create global impact. He left the self-development industry for finance so that he could better leverage his business acumen and communication skills.

Ever since high school, he aspired to sit at the intersection of the economy. Although he didn't know what the destination looked like, he set off in college to work with leaders across all industries.

Jesse graduated Florida State University with a degree in Entrepreneurship and Professional Sales. During his time at FSU, Jesse started up 2 companies and created 2 student organizations to catalyze the FSU entrepreneurial ecosystem. His speech at TEDx FSU is what propelled him toward a future of endless opportunity Jesse's career trajectory has not always been crystal clear. For years, Jesse struggled to align his passions and find the proper teams to work with. Many of the concepts in this book came about from his perceptions of operational inefficiencies throughout corporate America.

Jesse's commitment to society transcends "impact" and "financial abundance." He has a vision of what the world can look like, and he's going to stop at nothing to make it happen.

If you enjoyed this book, please go over to www.Amazon.com and write a review.

Made in the USA
Las Vegas, NV
08 March 2021